Multi-media

The Complete Guide

Multi-media
The Complete Guide

DORLING KINDERSLEY
LONDON · NEW YORK · SYDNEY · MOSCOW

A DORLING KINDERSLEY BOOK

1998 REVISED EDITION

Project Editor Anna Milner
Project Art Editor Tim Mann
Additional Designer Nigel Coath
Text Contributors Joanna Bawa, Angus Kennedy,
Anna Milner, David Pitchford, Bill Thompson
Picture Researcher Sam Ruston
Production Manager Ian Paton
Managing Editor Francis Ritter
Managing Art Editor Derek Coombes

1996 EDITION

Project Editors Joe Elliot, Tim Worsley
Project Art Editor Nigel Coath
Editors Brian Cooper, Susan Schlachter, John Watson
Editor-in-Chief Anthony Whitehorn
Senior Designer Stephen Cummiskey
Designers Tim Mann, Trond Wilhelmsen
Illustrators Coneyl Jay, Peter Scott, Matthew Wallis
Additional Illustrators Nigel Coath, Stephen Cummiskey, Tim Mann, Trond Wilhelmsen
Photographers Tony Buckley, Gary Ombler, Steve Gorton, Andy Crawford
Text Contributors David Bowen, George Cole, Brian Cooper, Joe Elliot,
Paul Glancey, Rupert Goodwins, Nina Hathway, Peter Jackson, Graeme Kidd,
Damien Noonan, Penelope Ody, Susan Schlachter, Steve Shipside,
John Watson, Sid Wells, Tim Worsley
Picture Researchers Ingrid Nilsson, Sam Ruston
Editorial Director Reg Grant
Design Director Tony Foo
Publisher Jonathan Reed

This edition copyright © 1998 Dorling Kindersley Limited, London

First published in Great Britain in 1996
by Dorling Kindersley Limited
9 Henrietta Street, London WC2E 8PS

Visit us on the World Wide Web at http://www.dk.com

ISBN 0 7513 0541 3

Colour Reproduction by Triffik Technology, London
Printed and bound in Spain by Artes Gráficas Toledo, S.A.
D.L.TO: 1014-1998

Preface

W E ARE LIVING IN THE MILLENNIUM OF the book, the century of cinema, and the decade of multimedia. The consequences of this are staggering. Our world is awash with information. We are confronted with a constant stream of new information and also a constant stream of new information technologies: multimedia, on-line multimedia, interactive television, virtual reality, the Internet, and so on.

Despite the rush of technology, however, multimedia may hold the key to simplifying the information age. By presenting words, sounds, pictures, animation, and film in an interactive way it allows us to choose our own paths through information. In this respect, it is similar to the natural ways we learn as young children. When we come into this world we are beautifully programmed – to crawl around, to touch things, to look at things, to hear things, to feel things. We do not need words, concepts, or a curriculum: we explore. It is said that in our first year we learn more than at any other time in our lives. This total interaction with information is what multimedia offers: in a multimedia environment you can learn naturally. And because multimedia creates worlds you can control, its potential to entertain and educate is enormous.

This fully revised edition of *Multimedia: the Complete Guide* is a comprehensive and detailed exploration of the entire multimedia phenomenon. It contains over 1,000 images, which reveal how multimedia works, how it is used, and how it is made. It examines the full range of multimedia applications – encyclopedias, interactive movies, in-flight entertainment, and so on – as well as the range of multimedia machines – computers, home consoles, and virtual reality equipment. The book reveals how multimedia text, sound, graphics, animation, and video are created and how they are built into an interactive whole. In addition, it explores the world of on-line multimedia, the Internet, and interactive television – as it is today and as it will be in the future.

Today, a child exploring a multimedia encyclopedia can discover – through words and sounds and moving pictures – how the agricultural revolution brought civilization to humankind. The same encyclopedia will illustrate interactively how the Industrial Revolution took us into the modern world. And future editions will reveal how the closing decades of this millennium marked the beginning of the information revolution.

Peter Kindersley

Peter Kindersley

CONTENTS

MULTIMEDIA SOFTWARE

HOW MULTIMEDIA COMPUTERS WORK

MULTIMEDIA MACHINES

HOW MULTIMEDIA IS MADE

MULTIMEDIA DOWN THE LINE

CHAPTER 5

INTRODUCTION

MULTIMEDIA MAY WELL BE THE most powerful educational tool yet invented, and it has the potential to become the ultimate in entertainment. The reason for this is twofold. First, as its name conveys, multimedia has the supreme advantage of combining many different types of media into one: text, pictures, animation, narration, video, and music. Second, it is interactive: the user does not receive the information passively, as when reading a book or watching television, but controls it, deciding which of the various avenues to explore and being able to jump forward, backward, or from one to another at will. This information can be controlled, accessed, and cross-referenced in a way that suits the user. Multimedia has serious applications too. It is becoming an important tool in the business world for training staff at a level and pace that suits each individual, and having a powerful influence in retail and trade. Multimedia will contribute to changes in the patterns of our daily lives, both at home and at work, in ways that we cannot yet predict.

MULTIMEDIA
In 1985, Microsoft called multimedia "the new papyrus."

A MULTIMEDIA REVOLUTION

There is another definition of multimedia, often spoken of in the same breath as the Internet or "information superhighway," that involves the merging of communications and media industries such as telephone, cable television, and movie companies. It is a vision of a vast network that will bring multimedia software, and assorted other services, into the home via telephone lines, fiber-optic cables, and even satellite. This vision is fast becoming reality.

However you define it, multimedia is having a huge impact on our lives. It might have been premature to label it "the new papyrus," as Microsoft did over a decade ago, but few now doubt that multimedia technology is set to play an equally revolutionary role.

DIGITAL DAYS

The key to this multimedia revolution is digitization – which means the conversion of all types of information, such as words, sound, pictures, video, and numbers, into a special code that electronic machines can recognize and understand.

The first type of machine to make use of digital information was the computer. "Information processors," which filled whole rooms, began to appear in large organizations in the 1950s; they were used to perform complex calculations, and could display only text and figures on screen.

Soon, simple digital graphics were appearing on computers; inevitably, the first programs to be run on the graphics-capable systems were games.

Technology moved on, and by the late seventies, video arcades were offering interactive multimedia that combined graphics and computer-generated sound in games such as *Space Invaders*.

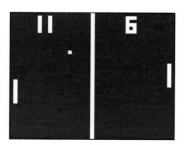

EARLY GRAPHICS
Computer graphics as they looked in 1972 in Atari's *Pong* tennis game.

DIGITAL DISTRACTIONS
Early arcade games such as *Battlezone* were the public's first taste of digital graphics.

Soon hobbyists were buying the first home computers and games consoles. Then, in 1981, IBM unveiled its first PC (personal computer), and the business world bought into computing wholesale. Few people, however, predicted the breakneck pace of growth and development that has characterized the computer industry ever since.

Today just about anything can be converted into digital code. A computer simply processes numbers and does not know or care whether those numbers represent a Mozart symphony, a Rembrandt self-portrait, or an accounting firm's five-year business plan. Multimedia home computers can now produce stunning 3-D graphics, photo-realistic pictures, movie footage, hi-fi sound, and breathtaking animation, while all the time they are just pushing figures.

Today's multimedia computers are at the forefront of a much bigger multimedia revolution, however – they are leading the move away from analog media machines towards digital ones.

PAINT BY NUMBERS
A digitized masterpiece is just another set of electronic code to a multimedia computer.

ANALOG INTO DIGITAL

FROM A TO D
Today's analog media machines will probably be superseded by digital ones.

Most of the media machines in homes today – for example, television sets, video recorders, radios, and most telephones – are analog. They deal with data that has been transmitted as varying electrical voltages, not as electronic code.

This is changing fast. Most cordless and cellular telephones already use digital technology. Radio and television stations are introducing digital broadcasting, and the videocassette recorder (VCR) is under threat from digital video. While the thought of connecting your telephone to your TV set or your computer to your VCR may seem absurd now, one day they may all be in the same box. As technology advances and the digitization of media proceeds apace, so the foundations of the multimedia revoltion are being laid.

A forerunner in the revolution is the CD (compact disc), which was invented to hold digital music. Now, as the CD-ROM, it carries multimedia data too.

CD-ROM DELIVERS

CD-ROM (Compact Disc Read-Only Memory) sprang directly from the music CD, and from the same set of parents – Sony and Philips. It was a logical step; after all, music CDs store a stream of electronic code that represents sound waves: replace that code with one that conveys digital pictures, text, animation, and so on, attach a modified CD player to a computer, and you have CD-ROM.

When CD-ROM first appeared in the mid-1980s, the storage capacity it offered the computer world seemed truly awesome. It could hold about 20 times more information than the hard disk of a typical desktop computer. To put that into perspective, a single CD-ROM can hold more than two complete sets of the Encyclopaedia Britannica, which is just the sort of quantity you need to produce high-quality multimedia. In fact, CD-ROM has been so successful a way to deliver multimedia products that now no home computer can be called truly complete without a CD-ROM drive.

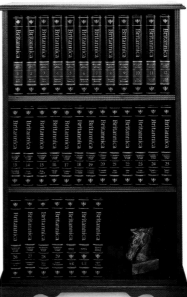

COMPACT KNOWLEDGE
The entire Encyclopaedia Britannica would fit twice on one CD-ROM.

YOUR OWN JOURNEY

Multimedia enables you to make your own way through information. This example from Dorling Kindersley's *Eyewitness Encyclopedia of Science 2.0* shows how it is possible to jump between related topics at will.

Going On-line
Clicking the globe icon on the main console takes you directly to the Science Online site on the World Wide Web.

Start Here
The scientist's console is the control center of the program. To explore the world of science, click on any image.

WORLDS TO EXPLORE

Just as you can flip from track to track on a music CD, you can navigate the data on a CD-ROM so that it becomes an interactive experience. Instead of following a linear path, as you would with a book, you can jump directly from one related entry to another as your interest takes you. Many of today's CD-ROM titles may even transport you in a single leap onto the Internet, opening up a huge on-line resource. And with the addition of graphics, animation, sound, or video, you can experience the full potential of multimedia.

Physics
Choosing the Force and Motion category under Physics brings up a visual menu. Clicking on any image takes you to a page containing a detailed article on that subject.

Video Clip
To watch a video clip about Weightlessness, click the Video button. The clip plays in a window and then returns to the page.

Making a Link
Click on the Galileo Galilei image in the See Also box to jump to a biography of the famous Italian scientist.

See Also
The See Also box displays a list of related topics.

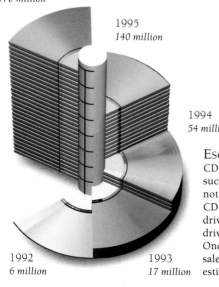

1996
170 million

1995
140 million

1994
54 million

1992
6 million

1993
17 million

ESCALATING SALES
CD-ROM was hardly an overnight success. Software companies would not risk the high costs of developing CD-ROM titles until more people had drives, but people were not buying drives until they saw more software. Once the deadlock eased, however, sales of CD-ROMs took off, as these estimated worldwide figures show.

INTERACTIVE ADVENTURES
Multimedia lets you explore information at your own pace. You can wander through an art gallery and choose which pictures to look at, what level of detail you require, and whether or not you want an expert spoken commentary. Or you could listen to a Beethoven symphony bar by bar, with the musical score shown on-screen and with extra annotations to point out the imagery and the repeated themes.

Multimedia does not stop at the edges of the real world either – from the cockpit of a jet aircraft or an X-Wing spacecraft you can fly through the virtual terrain of today's interactive games. Once information, real or imaginary, has been digitized and put on a CD-ROM or the Internet, it can form part of a spectacular interactive world of discovery.

A Stopgap Measure?

At the present time, CD-ROM is the most widely used medium for delivering multimedia. Software companies like it because once a title has been developed, discs are cheap to mass-produce. Consumers like it because of the new, exciting software it carries.

However, CD-ROM is not quite perfect for multimedia. The CD's musical roots mean that jumping from track to track and reading data off the disc both happen at a laid-back pace better suited to a music center than to the needs of interactive multimedia. Compared to the hard disk of any desktop computer, a CD-ROM drive is many times slower, and its capacity seems less and less dramatic. While it is true that one disc can hold a huge amount of text, the figures are not as impressive for graphics or video.

As we reach the limits of the single disc – some games titles occupy as many as seven discs – questions are being asked about the future of CD-ROM. Over the next few years the CD-ROM is likely to be superseded by high-density compact discs formats, such as digital video disc, which have fast data access times and the capacity to hold several complete movies. But some experts predict an even more radical future in which the CD will disappear altogether as soon as it becomes possible to send large quantities of data quickly over a worldwide communications network such as the Internet.

QUESTIONABLE FUTURE
Will CD-ROM survive, or will it be eclipsed by the Internet and on-line multimedia?

ON-LINE SERVICES
Services currently on trial include video-on-demand, video games, and on-line shopping.

THE INTERNET

IN CONTROL
This remote control for a TV puts interactive multimedia in the palm of your hand.

There are strong indications that the Internet will become the new storage medium for a lot of data currently held on CD-ROM. In the future you may not need to find space in your home for games, music CDs, CD-ROMs, or newspapers, as this information will be available on-line. Simply by connecting to a server, which could be located anywhere in the world, you will be able to access any of this data remotely – interactive multimedia on-line.

It is already possible to access a wide range of interactive services using the Internet. You can browse on-line research libraries, play games against opponents anywhere in the world, or purchase goods.

As communications technology advances and the amount of digital data that can be sent down a wire at high speed increases, the Internet will play an integral part in the realization of an information superhighway – a proposed high-speed communications network that will bring multimedia into the home through a socket in the wall.

The future will put you in control of your own path through a sophisticated range of interactive services, such as video and music on-demand and news broadcasts tailored to meet your own personal interests. We will not know for some time the exact direction that these services will take, but it is this vision of an interactive future that is driving the multimedia industry forward.

THE NOT-SO-SUPER HIGHWAY?

The wide range of promised interactive multimedia services is an exciting prospect, and it is no wonder that it stirs up such media interest. Yet, although the wheels of the information superhighway are already in motion, there is a long way to go before it fulfils its promise of delivering state-of-the-art multimedia into the home.

Every home will need a high-capacity link to a network of even higher capacity. Until recently many experts assumed that only fiber-optic cable would be fast enough to provide these links, requiring enormous investment. But standards in communications technology are constantly improving, providing ways to push more and more data down the existing copper wires owned by the telephone companies, so perhaps an entirely fiber-optic network may not be necessary after all. Even so, it will be a good five or ten years before all the services and equipment that will comprise the information superhighway are fully in place.

FUTURE MULTIMEDIA
In the not-too-distant future, many people will get their multimedia through a TV set and set-top, signal-decoder box.

TOO MUCH EQUIPMENT?

While the superhighway is still some way off and its exact nature is not yet clear, the one thing today's TV, telecommunications, and computer companies are all sure of is that their survival depends on being part of the action. With so many players all trying to get ahead and set the standard that the rest have to follow, it is possible that the home of the future will not have a single, all-in-one, on-line multimedia system but will instead have multiple sources of digital information – the games cartridge, CD-ROM, digital video disc, and a host of interactive TV services – along with a stack of decoder boxes, one for each type. If the digital media machines of the future are as incompatible as today's analog machines – so that you have to dial up one system to watch a movie, and another to find out more about an idea the film sparks off in your mind – perhaps the whole point of the digital revolution will have been missed.

Still, while the media companies of today rush to be the multimedia companies of tomorrow, all fighting for their own lane on the information superhighway, we may as well sit back and enjoy the ride – the interactive ride, that is – in the knowledge that, whatever it looks like when the dust finally does settle, multimedia is here to stay.

PRESENT-DAY MULTIMEDIA
There is a danger that our access to the information superhighway could require a mass of incompatible equipment from a host of competing multimedia companies, just as we have today.

HOW TO USE THIS BOOK

This book is designed for browsing rather than reading from cover to cover. The book's five chapters cover everything from multimedia software and what you can do with it to the wide range of multimedia machines and how they work, from a behind-the-scenes look at how multimedia titles are made to how on-line multimedia and the information superhighway will affect our lives. At the back of the book you will find a detailed glossary of terms and a comprehensive index. As an additional help, throughout the book certain key terms are highlighted as hotspots. Hotspots point you toward another section of the book where you will find more information on the subject.

To get you started, the outline below tells you what each chapter contains.

Hotspots
point you to
more information

1 MULTIMEDIA SOFTWARE
The first chapter looks at the different types of multimedia software and what you can do with them – from education, training, and reference titles to the games and entertainment classics.

2 HOW MULTIMEDIA COMPUTERS WORK
This chapter takes the lid off a multimedia computer to show how it works, following the passage of digital data from the CD-ROM, the mouse, and the keyboard to the screen and speakers.

3 MULTIMEDIA MACHINES
This chapter compares the major multimedia players, from the PC and the Apple Macintosh to the home consoles – the Saturn, the PlayStation, the Nintendo 64 – and on to the imaginary worlds of virtual-reality machines.

4 HOW MULTIMEDIA IS MADE
From the secrets of 3-D animators to the workings of the sound studio, this chapter gives you a guided tour of how today's state-of-the-art multimedia titles are made.

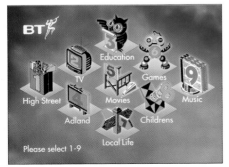

5 MULTIMEDIA DOWN THE LINE
The final chapter looks at the world of on-line multimedia – the Internet, the World Wide Web – and the services you can expect in the future: interactive TV, video-on-demand, and more.

What is interactive
multimedia – and
what can it do?
This chapter explores what is
meant by "interactivity" and
looks at the many different
kinds of multimedia software:
encyclopedias, interactive
museums, math teachers,
animated storybooks, games,
interactive movies, in-flight
entertainment, and more.

THE WORLD OF MULTIMEDIA

MULTIMEDIA SOFTWARE EMERGED in the mid-eighties, soon after the CD-ROM was invented. CD-ROM, with its vast storage capacity, has been compared in significance to paper, the printing press, and photography. By the early 1990s, the multimedia phenomenon was gathering momentum and attracting great media interest; by the mid 1990s multimedia software was finding its place on the Internet. Even if multimedia does not live up to all the hype, it is already a multibillion-dollar industry, creating hundreds of new titles each month. Many of these titles put computers to uses that could not have been anticipated when multimedia first took off.

Internet
For more on the Internet, see page 164

SOFTWARE FOR EVERYONE

Most of the multimedia titles produced today are designed for home use. These titles fall into three broad categories: reference, which brings the resources of the public library into the home; education, which supplements classroom schooling; and entertainment. Within each category, certain genres have been established: the cartoon adventure and the interactive movie, for example, are both well-defined strands of entertainment software. A fourth category, services, covers wider multimedia applications: in workplaces, public galleries, shopping malls, and even airplanes.

In retrospect, it is not hard to see why multimedia has been put to so many uses. Computers have become powerful enough to process enormous quantities of almost any type of information, from statistical databases to full-screen video sequences. And millions of people worldwide – all with different tastes and interests – now have access to computers and software delivered on CD-ROM or via the Internet. These factors have all contributed to the rich variety of multimedia titles shown here. On the pages that follow, each genre is explored in more detail.

Reference
Encyclopedias
Atlases
Leisure Titles
Museums
Hybrid Titles

HOME LIBRARY
Reference is an established and popular use for CD-ROM-based multimedia. Traditional reference books – such as encyclopedias and atlases – adapt well to multimedia. And, although early claims that multimedia heralded the "death of the book" seem exaggerated, multimedia encyclopedias now outsell printed ones.

Museums

Encyclopedias

Atlases

MULTIMEDIA CLASSROOM

Educational software has long had a role in schools, offering students structured learning exercises that they can carry out at their own pace. Multimedia's potential for entertainment has led to a new breed of software – known as "edutainment" – that promotes learning through play, creative activities, and adventure games.

Education

Early Learning
Storybooks
Math and Logic
Creativity Tools
Language Learning
Science

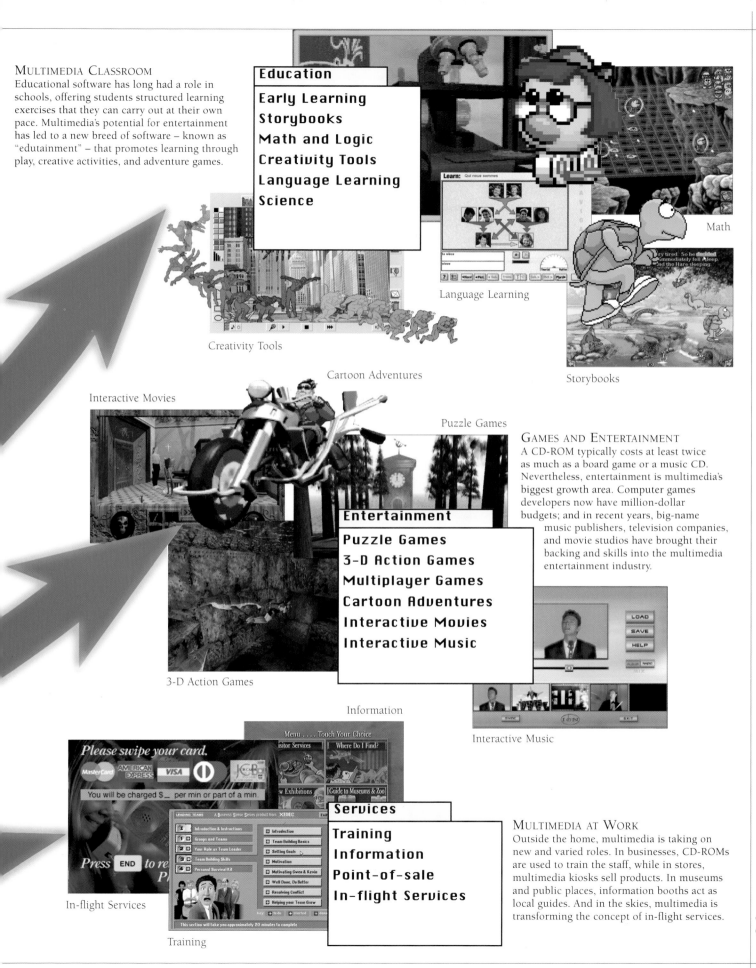

Math

Language Learning

Storybooks

Creativity Tools

Cartoon Adventures

Interactive Movies

Puzzle Games

GAMES AND ENTERTAINMENT

A CD-ROM typically costs at least twice as much as a board game or a music CD. Nevertheless, entertainment is multimedia's biggest growth area. Computer games developers now have million-dollar budgets; and in recent years, big-name music publishers, television companies, and movie studios have brought their backing and skills into the multimedia entertainment industry.

Entertainment

Puzzle Games
3-D Action Games
Multiplayer Games
Cartoon Adventures
Interactive Movies
Interactive Music

3-D Action Games

Information

Interactive Music

Services

Training
Information
Point-of-sale
In-flight Services

In-flight Services

Training

MULTIMEDIA AT WORK

Outside the home, multimedia is taking on new and varied roles. In businesses, CD-ROMs are used to train the staff, while in stores, multimedia kiosks sell products. In museums and public places, information booths act as local guides. And in the skies, multimedia is transforming the concept of in-flight services.

How Interactivity Works

Multimedia software is ideal for presenting the varied types of information (text, animation and narrations, pictures, music, video) that can be stored on a computer or CD-ROM. But the most important part of the multimedia experience is interactivity: not merely being able to access the available information but also having the opportunity to navigate through it, play with it, and perhaps even create something new from it. The way that multimedia software presents information and enables you to interact with it is called its "user interface." The interface must do two things. First, it must tell you what is available and what it can do. Second, it must provide you with a way of making a choice from the options presented. In most multimedia titles, this is achieved through the use of what is known as "hypermedia."

Hypermedia

Many reference titles open with a main control screen, which is the heart of the user interface. From here you can explore the title. This might involve reading text, listening to music, watching movie clips, and so on. Some of these words, sounds, and pictures will be interactive and are known as "hypermedia." Hypermedia can be recognized by two characteristics. First, they enable you to respond to them, and they will respond to you. For example, if you choose a word you might be taken to other, related words; or if you choose a picture you might be switched to another part of the title. Second, hypermedia present choices that are multilinear – they offer many paths through the same information. The two forms of hypermedia most commonly used in multimedia are hypertext and hotspots.

INTERACTIVE BOOKS
Voyager's *Expanded Book* series takes popular novels and adds simple interactivity to the text. Although not strictly multimedia – they do not include sound or moving pictures – they are good examples of how hypertext can be used.

Hypertext

Text-based titles often make the best use of hypertext. With hypertext, every word is "live," which means that you can select or interact with it in some way – exactly how depends on the way the title has been designed. In Voyager's *Zen and the Art of Motorcycle Maintenance*, you can highlight any word or passage that interests you, copy whole passages for inclusion in a word processor document, or type notes into the margin without defacing the text. And when you choose a particular word, you can see a list of all the pages where it occurs and jump straight to any of them.

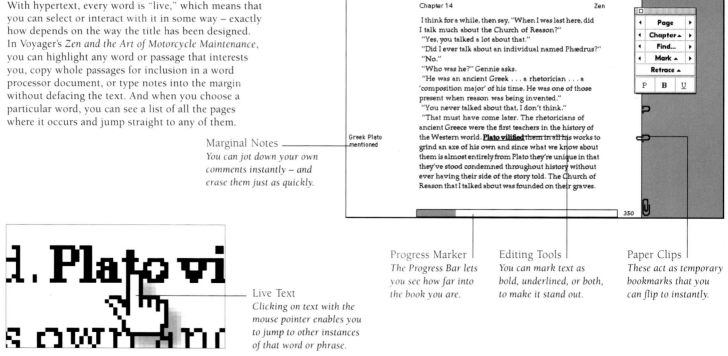

Marginal Notes
You can jot down your own comments instantly – and erase them just as quickly.

Live Text
Clicking on text with the mouse pointer enables you to jump to other instances of that word or phrase.

Progress Marker
The Progress Bar lets you see how far into the book you are.

Editing Tools
You can mark text as bold, underlined, or both, to make it stand out.

Paper Clips
These act as temporary bookmarks that you can flip to instantly.

Point and Click

The single most useful tool for the multimedia computer user is the mouse and its on-screen pointer, or cursor. In most multimedia titles a small pointer on the screen – most often in the shape of a hand or an arrow – follows the movements of the mouse. Choices are presented on-screen as words or pictures, and choosing between them is simple: you just point with the mouse and click the mouse button. Home console owners generally use a joypad to control the pointer instead, but the principle is the same.

Bioforge
The robot hero's hand in Origin's Bioforge *becomes the pointer for menu selections.*

POINTER POWER

Pointers take many forms, even within the same program. Different pointer shapes are used to indicate, for example, when the pointer is over a hotspot, or when the program is pausing to load new data. This gives the user important feedback about his or her actions.

Moving Pointers
Some titles have animated cursors, such as this beckoning skeletal hand from Trilobyte's 7th Guest, *used to indicate a direction.*

HOTSPOTS

Voyager's *Making Maus*, like most multimedia titles, makes extensive use of hotspots. A hotspot is usually a button or picture that reacts when you select it – by taking you to another part of the title, for example. Most hotspots are revealed by exploring the screen with the mouse and observing where the pointer or image changes. Another type of hotspot is hot text – a word or phrase that appears in a different color from the main text to show that it is live. Not all hotspots declare themselves, however; sometimes you have to click around the screen to find them.

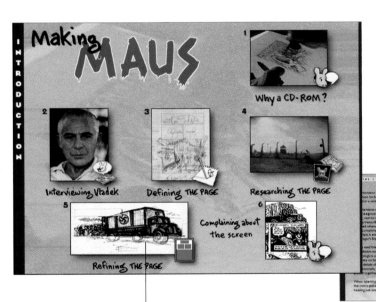

Dynamic Link
Hotspots often jump you to another screen. This action is known as a dynamic link. Here, one of the hotspots leads to a video and a transcript of an interview.

New Depths to the Page
The contents page is presented as a set of hotspot pictures. Each of these rectangles takes you to a different section of the title.

INTERFACIAL DIFFERENCES

A given subject presents different opportunities for interactive multimedia. Here, four titles that show how the human body works reveal some of the many different approaches possible.

Introduction

Page Layout

Background Research

Pencil Artwork

Multimedia Conversion

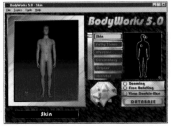

Softkey's *Body Works*

Dorling Kindersley's *The Ultimate Human Body*

IVI Publishing's *What is a Bellybutton?*

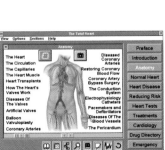

Mayo Clinic's *The Total Heart*

THE HOME LIBRARY

MULTIMEDIA REFERENCE TITLES can be used to access information in ways that would be impossible with printed books. Not only can the designers incorporate animations, videos, sound, and speech to enhance the presentation of written information, they can also provide hypertext and hypermedia links that allow the user to search for specific information or explore a topic more generally. The sophisticated "search engines" that allow you to embark on a fascinating voyage of discovery in multimedia reference titles are continually being refined and developed to allow easier access to the wealth of knowledge stored on these discs.

DIGITAL ENCYCLOPEDIAS

Encyclopedias have existed for almost 2,000 years. The Roman scholar Pliny the Elder's *Historia Naturalis* was the first, completed in AD 97. Multivolume printed editions, such as those published by Encyclopaedia Britannica or the *Academic American Encyclopedia*, have been used in schools and homes as reference sources throughout the 20th century. But the power of CD-ROM to store enormous amounts of information that can be searched in an almost infinite number of ways was quickly harnessed by encyclopedia publishers. As the multimedia CD-ROM revolution got under way, encyclopedia publishers stepped in, and by the mid-1990s most of the major printed encyclopedias had been released as CD-ROM titles.

MICROSOFT ENCARTA
Encarta uses menus that slide down onto the screen when the mouse is moved toward buttons or toolbars. When the Pinpointer search tool first appears, it contains an alphabetical listing of all the articles on the disc. *Encarta* also offers an adventure-style quiz game in which you travel through a maze in search of a princess, making progress by answering questions correctly.

Photographs and Illustrations
There are over 8,000 photographs and illustrations included in Encarta. *This one is a photograph of Jupiter taken by the Hubble Space Telescope; it shows the dark impact marks made on the planet by fragments of Comet Shoemaker-Levy 9.*

Outline
The Outline panel shows the main headings of an article together with the media elements it contains.

Immediate Access
Once you have made a selection from the Related Articles list, the new article is displayed immediately.

More Information
The More Information button brings up a list of options that will widen the scope of your search, such as going on-line or viewing related articles.

Areas and Categories
All Encarta's *information is classified into Areas of Interest and Categories. When you select an Area of Interest, Pinpointer lists all the Categories for you.*

Annotating
You can annotate or simply mark an article, using notemarks, which can be called up at any time.

Virtual Tours
This feature lets you step inside and explore world-famous buildings.

Timeline
A timeline places historical events in a wider context by showing what else was taking place at the same time in different parts of the world.

Copying Text
The Word Processor button opens a word processing program, which you can use to copy Encarta's articles for future reference.

Browsing Encarta
You can wander casually through a whole range of subjects.

Media Gallery
To list all examples of the different media, open this Gallery.

MindMaze
A fully interactive adventure game lets you test your knowledge.

Features
Media Features ▶
Online Features ▶
Tools ▶
⬧ Virtual Tours
⬌ InterActivities
🔊 Collages
▦ Media Gallery
☝ Topic Trails
Timeline
🌍 Atlas
🐍 MindMaze

Features
Media Features ▶
Online Features ▶
Tools ▶
🖼 Dictionary
📇 Research Organizer
📓 NoteMark
🔤 Browse Panel
📄 Word Processor

Hubble Space Telescope (HST), the first general-purpose orbiting observatory. Launched on April 24, 1990, the Hubble Space Telescope is named after the American astronomer Edwin P. Hubble. The HST makes observations in the visible and ultraviolet regions of the electromagnetic spectrum (*See* Electromagnetic Radiation). The primary mirror of the HST has a diameter of 94.5 in (2.4 m), and the optics of the telescope are designed so that when making a visible-light observation, the telescope can theoretically resolve astronomical objects that are an angular distance of 0.05 arcsecond apart. For

Atlas
Encarta includes an atlas that enables you to select a continent or country and then zoom in on a more detailed area, such as the state of Washington (left). Local views are also available, such as the Seattle skyline (above).

Animation
In a number of Encarta's articles, animation is used to explain complex phenomena. Here, an animation of the solar system shows the planets orbiting the sun.

Pinpointer
The Pinpointer locates topics and also contains features such as the ability to select all uses of one medium, for example, pictures or sounds.

Interactivity
By selecting the InterActivities icon on the Pinpointer's Media Gallery, you can experiment with several interactive screens. One, for example, enables you to change the position and orbital velocity of the moon.

Video Clips
Encarta's coverage of historic and world events is enhanced by a number of video clips. This one shows the Hubble Space Telescope undergoing repairs. The sound track records conversations between the astronauts and the ground-control center.

ONE-SUBJECT ENCYCLOPEDIAS

General encyclopedias have long been a multimedia standard, but now an increasing number of titles cover just one subject. Single-subject encyclopedias have two advantages over the general sort: first, being narrower in scope, they can go into much more detail; and second, they often present information in a more interesting way. The way a title presents information, its "look and feel," is known as its interface. General encyclopedias include so many different types of information that they have to use all-purpose interfaces, which are often fairly bland. One-subject titles, however, can build information into a graphical world specially created to entice the user into it. The example shown is Dorling Kindersley's *Eyewitness Encyclopedia of Nature 2.0*, where you can find out about the natural world by looking through a microscope, tapping on a barometer, opening specimen drawers, and spinning a globe.

FISH POSTER
The posters on the main console (see below) offer one of many ways into the body of the encyclopedia. In this case, each picture takes you to an entry for a major type of fish. From there you begin a journey of discovery, leaping from entry to entry as the mood takes you.

Graphical
For more on graphics, see page 130

Pick Your Subject
Choosing one of the fish on the poster calls up an encyclopedia entry on that type of fish.

INFORMATION CENTER
The main screen of the *Encyclopedia of Nature* is a naturalist's console, complete with spinning globe, drawers, reference books, and other artifacts. This acts as a pictorial contents page – every object represents a different subject area or activity. The graphical interface encourages exploration and offers many ways into the encyclopedia's body of information.

Fossil
This takes you to a time-line of the prehistoric era and subject entries about life before humans.

Globe
You can rotate the globe and zoom in to explore different habitats – tropical rain forest, for example, or a coral reef in the Pacific Ocean.

Animal Vision
The binoculars show comparisons of human and animal vision.

Nature Online
This globe takes you directly to the Nature Online *site on the Internet.*

Radio
This plays a selection of bird calls – from contact to alarm calls – for a variety of species.

Barometer
Tapping on different sections of the barometer gives you information on the seasons, oceans, climatic regions, and the natural elements.

Index
You can search the entire encyclopedia, or only those entries that contain audio, video, or animation.

Microscope
The microscope reveals the world of miniature life.

Green Book
This book opens to tell you about environmental issues. From any of its pages, you can move to related entries in the rest of the encyclopedia.

Classification
This area enables you to look up information according to major classifications, such as plants, animals, or fungi.

Specimen Drawers
These drawers pull out to reveal specimens of different animal and plant species.

Main Entry
Much of the information in the Encyclopedia of Nature is contained in the subject entry pages, which combine written and spoken information with pictures, sound recordings, animation sequences, video clips, and cross-references to other parts of the encyclopedia.

Cross-references
The See Also box points to a set of related but distinct topics – from here you can learn about the nature of fish, their habitat, and how they coexist with other forms of life.

Underwater Habitat
This coral reef scene shows a number of plant and animal species in their natural habitat. You can move about the habitat to explore it in more detail. The screen also acts as a starting point for further exploration.

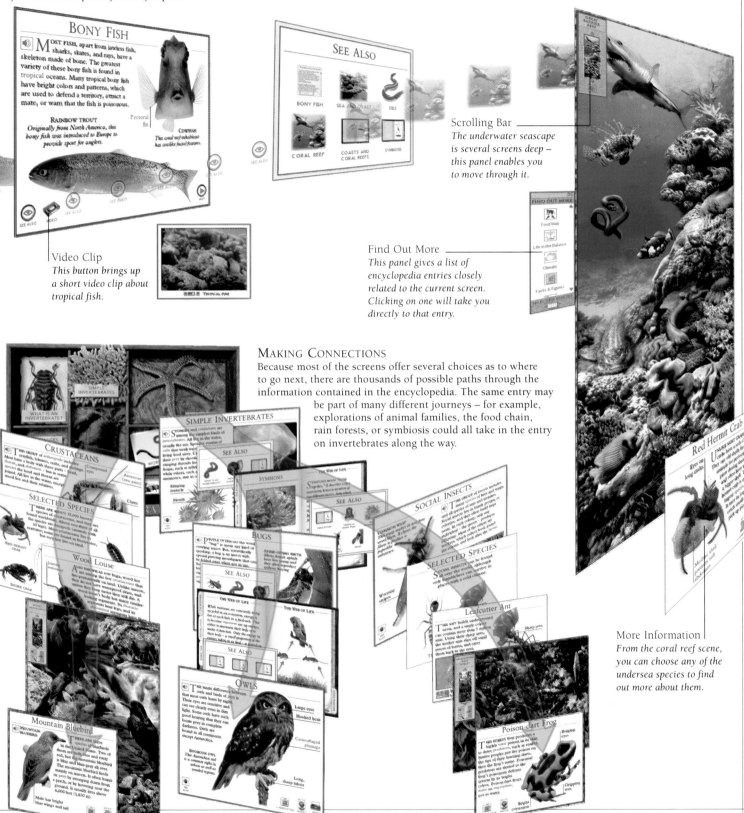

Scrolling Bar
The underwater seascape is several screens deep – this panel enables you to move through it.

Video Clip
This button brings up a short video clip about tropical fish.

Find Out More
This panel gives a list of encyclopedia entries closely related to the current screen. Clicking on one will take you directly to that entry.

MAKING CONNECTIONS
Because most of the screens offer several choices as to where to go next, there are thousands of possible paths through the information contained in the encyclopedia. The same entry may be part of many different journeys – for example, explorations of animal families, the food chain, rain forests, or symbiosis could all take in the entry on invertebrates along the way.

More Information
From the coral reef scene, you can choose any of the undersea species to find out more about them.

BROWSE THE WORLD

One of the most common reference books in the home is the atlas. Multimedia atlases present the same information in a more dynamic and involving way. Navigating around the world is made easy and every country is brought to life with multimedia features such as sound, animations, satellite and time-lapse photography, and video clips. With a good multimedia atlas you search for a place-name and find yourself at its map location in seconds. Alternatively, you might find yourself taking a trip from Andorra to Australia or from Zagreb to Zanzibar simply because desktop traveling can be so addictive.

MULTIMEDIA ATLASES

Like the book atlas, the multimedia version contains maps, illustrations, tables, and statistical data relating to the whole world, as well as to regions and countries. Multimedia's unique twist is that it uses sound, video, and animation to present this information more vividly. It also allows the user to make a large number of choices about the way each map is displayed.

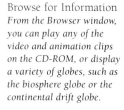

CONTROL THE WORLD

With many titles, you can decide how much detail and what kind of details you want to see on screen. The scale of maps can be adjusted using zoom buttons. You can also choose the features that appear on the maps, or you can add new locations.

Most multimedia titles contain large databases of statistical information. This information can be very wide-ranging – from data on total urban populations to the number of radios per thousand people in any country. You can usually display and print the answers to any query in a number of different ways.

Browse for Information
From the Browser window, you can play any of the video and animation clips on the CD-ROM, or display a variety of globes, such as the biosphere globe or the continental drift globe.

Climate Globes
The Wind Patterns globe is one of several globes that show climatic information.

World Clock
Here, you can enter a time-zone, date, and time to see the fall of night and day at that time.

Extinction Globe
This globe shows some of Earth's endangered species. You can click on any species to find out more.

Presenting Complex Statistics

Presentation can affect how one absorbs statistical information. Here you see examples of a scatter chart, ranking table, line chart, and globe chart – all relating to the world's population since 1950.

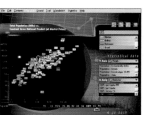

Scatter Chart

Ranking Table

Line Chart

Global Population Chart

USING THE 3D ATLAS

The main screen of Creative Wonders' *3D Atlas* features a globe and a find box. You can rotate the three-dimensional globe about any axis and zoom in to see individual countries or regions in more detail. You can also specify the type or amount of details to be displayed: for example, grid lines for latitude and longitude, cities, mountains, ocean depths. In addition, you can mark places that are significant to you with map pins and include text and pictures that you can view whenever you come back to the location in future.

"Find" Feature
As well as instituting a search for a particular location, you can specify features to be displayed in the list: for example, rivers or volcanoes.

Video Clips
3D Atlas contains a number of related video clips and animations. These include documentary videos about major environmental issues, such as acid rain and overfishing, and animated fly-throughs of different biomes, such as rain forest, tundra, and savanna.

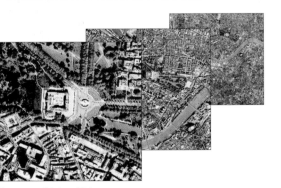

Focus on Major Cities
You can zoom in on satellite images of six major cities: Bombay, London, Moscow, New York, San Francisco, and Tokyo. This example shows London, with Buckingham Palace in the center.

Navigate the Globe
The main screen gives you several ways of navigating the globe. You can point to any area and zoom in via the plus button.

LEISURE PURSUITS

Leisure titles are among the fastest expanding multimedia sales areas. Books for the hobbyist and the enthusiast have always comprised a large part of publishing, and this strong market is being tapped for its multimedia potential. Books can offer a great deal, but more through the range of information they cover on any one subject than through flexibility and presentation, and it is precisely in this area of presentation that multimedia has the advantage.

TITLE FIGHT

It is in the area of leisure or lifestyle titles that multimedia is beginning to emerge as a viable alternative to traditional publishing. The range of subjects now available includes massage, beauty, and food; sports from golf to basketball; more practical pursuits such as carpentry; and hobbies such as photography, guitar playing, and astrology. As demand increases, so will the supply and variety of titles. Increasing specialization will also occur as the market grows and costs come down. Here, we take a look at Microsoft's *Cinemania*, *Music Central*, and *Wine Guide*.

Cinemania Online
Up-to-the-minute articles and reviews can be accessed on-line.

Cast Lists
The complete cast is available for the more important movies.

Reviews
Each movie listed by Cinemania is accompanied by at least one review to provide an idea of the quality and subject of the production.

CINEMANIA

The contents of Microsoft's *Cinemania* are accessed by first selecting from the categories: Movies, People, or Topics. In addition to the functions illustrated here, there is also a Gallery option that lists all the movies for which either stills, clips, music, or dialogue are available; a List Maker to record movies for future viewing; a Tours function that offers guided tours on specific movie themes; and an Awards option showing all Academy awards and nominations made since the prizes were established in 1927.

Dialogue Option
A short piece of dialogue is available for a number of movies included in Cinemania.

Movie Clip
For the major movies, a short clip lasting about 60 seconds can be viewed.

Biographies
More than 4,000 people connected with movies are included in Cinemania's biographical section. A photograph and a filmography are usually provided for the actors.

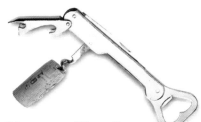

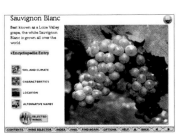

MICROSOFT WINE GUIDE

The *Wine Guide* covers all aspects of wine. Its pivotal feature is the extensive use of video clips of wine expert Oz Clarke, who light-heartedly presents the sometimes overserious world of wine.

Grape Profiles
Several hundred grape varieties are covered; and the characteristics of the 12 classic varieties are described in detail.

Worldwide Wine
The World Atlas of Wine contains maps of the 12 major wine-producing areas. The maps are interactive and contain information about geography, history, and grape varieties.

Reading the Label
A number of different wine labels are included; each one has several different areas highlighted, for which detailed explanations are available.

Team Pick
Open the Team Pick to read an in-depth feature on a recommended album. Each time the disc is used, the featured album changes.

MUSIC CENTRAL

Microsoft's *Music Central* is an encyclopedia of modern music. As well as the features shown here, it has a Suggestions function that helps you discover which artists are likely to appeal to you; and detailed biographies and discographies for all the artists featured on the disc.

Celebrity Tours
Music Central *offers a variety of theme Tours, in which different celebrities present an overview of topics such as Jazz and Rock'n'Roll.*

Searching
With the Find tool you can search by topic, artist, or album. You can further reduce the scope of a search using additional criteria such as country, musical genre, or era.

INTERACTIVE MUSEUMS

Visiting a modern museum or art gallery is perhaps the original multimedia experience – a combination of many of the elements that have made CD-ROM-based multimedia so successful. The exhibits in a museum are accompanied by written information, visual displays, and sometimes video presentations, and you can listen to expert commentary from a tour guide or on cassette. In addition, the exhibits are so arranged that you can browse through them and explore the information in your own way. Because museums so successfully combine various media in this way, they have given multimedia producers a useful model on which to base one-subject encyclopedia titles.

THE MUSEUM COMES TO YOU

Museums house the world's finest collections of antiquities and art treasures – their one disadvantage is the need for travel. With multimedia, however, you can see the Mona Lisa in the Louvre in Paris and the Smithsonian's dinosaur collection in Washington, DC, during the same afternoon. By combining photographs of the exhibits with detailed written and spoken information in a setting that imitates the real museum building, a multimedia museum can give the user a sense of actually visiting a collection.

ARTIFICIAL MUSEUMS

A multimedia title does not have to be based on a real museum, however. Using 3-D graphics, multimedia architects can construct a "virtual" museum building that exists only inside the computer. The user can wander through the imaginary building, stopping to take in and interact with the exhibits along the way. The example shown here, Dorling Kindersley's *Eyewitness Virtual Reality Cat*, combines a realistic museum interior with interactive exhibits to re-create the experience of visiting a museum.

3-D graphics
For more on 3-D graphics, see page 136

VIRTUAL MUSEUM
Dorling Kindersley's *Eyewitness Virtual Reality Cat* presents an artificial museum in the shape of an eye. The title enables you to walk through a realistic 3-D model building complete with museum-like displays. Here, the museum floor plan and two of the many 3-D walls are shown.

NAVIGATOR

Instant Navigation
The navigator shows you a map of the museum (right) from which you can jump instantly to any exhibit.

Walking Through
As in a real museum, you can wander through the rooms and corridors to choose the exhibits you want to look at.

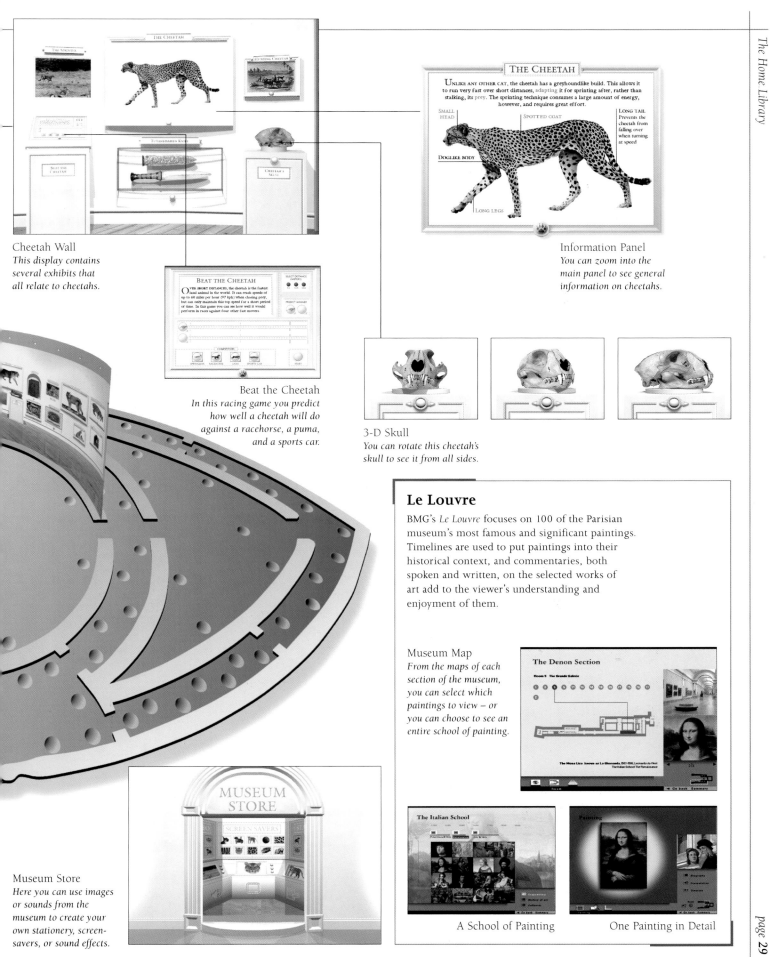

THE CHEETAH

UNLIKE ANY OTHER CAT, the cheetah has a greyhoundlike build. This allows it to run very fast over short distances, adapting it for sprinting after, rather than stalking, its prey. The sprinting technique consumes a large amount of energy, however, and requires great effort.

SMALL HEAD
LONG TAIL Prevents the cheetah from falling over when turning at speed
SPOTTED COAT
DOGLIKE BODY
LONG LEGS

Cheetah Wall
This display contains several exhibits that all relate to cheetahs.

Information Panel
You can zoom into the main panel to see general information on cheetahs.

BEAT THE CHEETAH

Beat the Cheetah
In this racing game you predict how well a cheetah will do against a racehorse, a puma, and a sports car.

3-D Skull
You can rotate this cheetah's skull to see it from all sides.

Le Louvre

BMG's *Le Louvre* focuses on 100 of the Parisian museum's most famous and significant paintings. Timelines are used to put paintings into their historical context, and commentaries, both spoken and written, on the selected works of art add to the viewer's understanding and enjoyment of them.

Museum Map
From the maps of each section of the museum, you can select which paintings to view – or you can choose to see an entire school of painting.

The Denon Section

Museum Store
Here you can use images or sounds from the museum to create your own stationery, screen-savers, or sound effects.

The Italian School

A School of Painting

One Painting in Detail

HYBRID TITLES

World Wide Web
For more on the World Wide Web, see page 166

THE RAPID EXPANSION of the World Wide Web during the last few years has had a huge impact on CD-ROM multimedia publications, and many of today's state-of-the-art titles owe as much to the Web as they do to CD-ROM. From multimedia encyclopedias through to children's edutainment discs, more and more of today's titles are being produced as "hybrid" CD-ROMs. Hybrid titles combine traditional multimedia software with features that transport users onto the Internet, where they can embark on an interactive voyage of discovery on the World Wide Web.

MAKING THE CONNECTION

Before the advent of the World Wide Web, multimedia publishers had to rely on CD-ROM for distributing information. Now, with new channels of communication opened up by the Internet, developers are increasingly using on-line content to supplement information contained on their CD-ROMs. In this way, they can provide a solid content base, on a disc, as well as a stream of up-to-date information that users can access on-line. Hybrid CDs create an interface between these two pools of information, enabling users who have an Internet account to access associated on-line information directly from the CD-ROM. Many hybrid titles supply software for connecting to the Internet, together with information explaining how to go about it.

Internet account
For more on Internet accounts, see page 165

The titles shown here show some of the different ways in which hybrid titles utilize the Web. Some provide content you just view online; some post content that you download and then view via the CD-ROM's user interface; others merely provide links to sites that, though useful for reference, are not an integral part of the product.

ON-LINE MAGAZINES
The Web site associated with Dorling Kindersley's *Eyewitness Virtual Reality Dinosaur Hunter* is presented in the style of an on-line magazine. Users access *Dino Online* via a console on the CD-ROM. The site offers interactive forums and a constantly changing supply of projects and information.

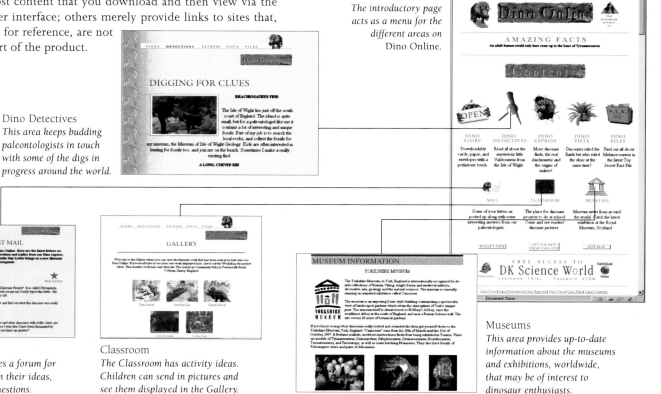

Dino Online
The introductory page acts as a menu for the different areas on Dino Online.

Dino Detectives
This area keeps budding paleontologists in touch with some of the digs in progress around the world.

Mail
Dino Mail provides a forum for children to send in their ideas, comments, and questions.

Classroom
The Classroom has activity ideas. Children can send in pictures and see them displayed in the Gallery.

Museums
This area provides up-to-date information about the museums and exhibitions, worldwide, that may be of interest to dinosaur enthusiasts.

On-line Features
Encarta's on-line features are easily accessible from the main screen. You do not need to enter the body of the encyclopedia.

UPDATING THE HOME LIBRARY

Microsoft's *Encarta* uses the Internet in a variety of ways, both to enhance and update the content of the encyclopedia. *Encarta's* on-line features enable users to download new articles for their CD-ROM; connect to the *Encarta Online* Web site for up-to-date information; or explore a host of independent Web sites that relate to information contained in the encyclopedia.

ONLINE FEATURES

Yearbook
browse new and updated articles

Web Links
explore the latest links between encarta and the web

Downloads
get the latest article updates and web links

Encarta Online
connect to encarta's web site for online features

World Wide Web Tips
learn what the world wide web is and how to connect to it

Downloads

Update Encarta — New Yearbook article updates and Web Links are available. To update your encyclopedia, click Update Encarta. All available Yearbook article updates and Web Links will be downloaded and integrated into Encarta Encyclopedia.

Troubleshoot — If you encounter problems, click Troubleshoot.

Yearbook
The CD-ROM's Yearbook provides the interface for viewing articles downloaded from the Web. The articles combine throughout the year to form a day-by-day diary of major world events.

Encarta Online
Among other things, Encarta Online keeps users in touch with new products and upgrades, and has a section offering technical support.

Downloads
Each time you visit the Downloads page, the CD-ROM checks to see how many new articles are available for you to download to your hard disk from Encarta Online.

Web Links
This section brings up a list of Web sites, organized according to Encarta's main subject categories, that can be accessed directly from the CD-ROM by clicking on the appropriate link.

ON-LINE ACCESS

Encarta's on-line features can be accessed from several places, not just the main screen. When viewing any article, you can find out if there are related on-line links by clicking the More Information button.

More Information Button

Related Web Sites
This box displays a list of Web sites related to the current article. Selecting one connects you to that site automatically.

Grand Canyon Site
You can reach this site via the Web Links or Grand Canyon article.

The Multimedia Classroom

ALL WORK AND NO PLAY makes Jack a dull boy, so the saying goes – but with many current educational multimedia titles, Jack would have difficulty telling the two activities apart. Many of the most popular "edutainment" titles combine elements of entertainment and education so effectively that younger children are unaware that they are learning. The best educational titles have learned some valuable lessons from games titles – they are packed with colorful animations, sound, video, and humor. Such titles are equally accessible to very young children, if they are helped by an adult, and to older children, who can explore the new worlds on-screen at their own pace. Edutainment is now an important consideration when a family buys a multimedia computer.

Playing and Learning

Much of a young child's learning takes place through the inter-activity of play: amusing himself or herself with toys and other objects, and experimenting with them, and taking part with others in games. This is well known by the producers of educational multimedia software for young children, and they have fashioned their products accordingly. Titles in this area fall into two broad groups. Some help to build skills in a specific subject area, such as spelling or math. Others are more open-ended and help children to develop their thinking skills; this kind of program is often described as "a gymnasium for the mind."

Preschool Activities

Jumpstart Kindergarten from Knowledge Adventure is a collection of three kinds of preschool educational activities which can be broadly categorized as simple learning, problem solving, and developing creativity. Simple learning activities present essential, basic information, such as the letters of the alphabet, simple sequences of numbers, and the days of the week. Problem-solving activities usually require the child to recognize relationships between objects; for example, the child may be asked to place in order a number of dolls according to their relative size, or a series of numbered blocks in ascending or descending order. Creative activities invite the child to express himself or herself – for example, by constructing simple sentences or by choosing colors for the pictures in the paint-box exercise.

Jumpstart Kindergarten

Like many multimedia titles for the preschool age group, the on-screen environment of Knowledge Adventure's *Jumpstart Kindergarten* is very lively, with sounds and animations working to keep the child's attention at all times. The main screen represents a classroom. By clicking on the relevant parts of the screen, the child can take part in a variety of activities. These teach telling the time, basic counting and geometry, reading, and language skills.

See How They Run
Choosing a number on the mat will bring the same number of mice scurrying from the mouse hole. This activity teaches simple counting.

An Exercise in Size
This activity involves placing a set of Russian dolls in order of size. A star appears below any doll that is placed in the correct position.

Learning by Numbers
Here the task is to arrange the blocks in numerical order. This teaches the child about number relationships.

Perfect Teacher

Mr. Hopsalot – the cartoon rabbit who acts as guide and teacher figure for the kindergarten – regularly offers instructions and advice on how to use the program and its activities. He also provides plenty of encouragement and praise when it is needed.

Follow That Hamster
Inside the cage, a hamster sunbathes – but not for long. Soon he disappears, leaving a clue behind him. By following this clue, the child will find him within one of the other activities.

Telling the Time
"10 o'clock AM: I play in the schoolyard." The animated clock teaches the relationship between the time and daily activities.

Pick a Flower
This door leads outside to the garden where Mr. Hopsalot is planting flowers. Here the activity is to name the next flower in a simple sequence.

Just for Fun
Under the sink lurks a plumber – some animations and sounds just make the kindergarten a lively place in which to be.

Choosing Colors
For this paint-box activity the child first identifies the odd one out in a group of three images. He or she then uses the palette on the left of the screen to color the images.

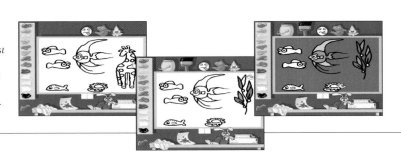

CHILDREN'S STORIES

Stories for children will never be the same again thanks to multimedia and the interactivity of CD-ROM. Multimedia children's storybooks are interactive versions of printed children's books, offering their users new worlds to explore and enjoy. They are simple to use, let children progress through a story at their own pace, and, best of all, can be very effective in helping a child learn to read.

LEARNING TO READ

Most multimedia children's storybooks work on the principle that entertainment and education can make a powerful combination: children usually encounter a variety of humorous characters who pop up to embellish the main story with amusing diversions; and at the same time children learn to read by following the text on the screen as it is read out by a narrator, and by watching short animations that illustrate the meaning of different words or phrases.

LIVING BOOKS

Broderbund's *Living Books* is one of the best children's series on CD-ROM. Each title is based on a popular story and consists of a series of animated screens that take children through the tale. The opening screen offers children two options: "Read to Me" lets them sit passively through the story as it is narrated; "Let Me Play" means they can play interactively with the characters on screen. Apart from their entertainment value, the titles also help children to recognize words. You can see how it all works here, with a screen from *The Tortoise and the Hare*. The scene opens with the tired Hare slowing down and taking a rest under a tree.

Secret Password
Choose the door in the tree and a young mouse walks up, knocks on the door, and asks "Can I come in?" But she needs a secret password. After three wrong guesses she realizes the password is "Can I come in, please?"

THE TORTOISE AND THE HARE
Based on Aesop's fable, Broderbund's *The Tortoise and the Hare* takes this classic story and enhances it with multimedia interactivity. After hearing a part of the story read aloud, children can click on almost anything on the screen to discover a hidden surprise.

Grammar Lessons

Two of the screens concentrate on verbs and prepositions. The Hare performs a series of actions, while the Tortoise encounters some obstacles he has to get over. Children can click on each word, hear it spoken, and see the relevant meaning through an animated sequence.

Skipping
With typical energy, the Hare illustrates the word "skip."

Uphill
The Tortoise sweats as he struggles to demonstrate the meaning of the word "uphill."

Highlighted Words
Whether a child chooses to listen passively to the story or to play with it interactively, the words on each screen are read out by a narrator. Each word can be highlighted using the cursor, allowing the child to hear it read aloud again.

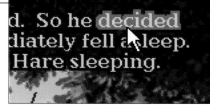

THE TORTOISE
As the hero of the story, the Tortoise defies all odds by winning the race through slow but steady progress.

Tarzan in the Trees
Click in the trees, and a young bear swings through the branches, yodeling like Tarzan. He crashes through the treehouse window, reappears at the front door with a saucepan jammed firmly over his head, then reels down the stairs before disappearing out of the left-hand side of the screen.

Dinosaur Antics
The right bank of the river is home to a dinosaur who tramps noisily around the river, calls out in an unexpected soprano, then smiles sheepishly before disappearing off the screen.

SIMON THE STORYTELLER
The story is narrated by Simon, a crow in red sneakers. He appears in each scene to read the text, and even adds his own asides to the story.

Fishy Games
Even the water holds a surprise; click in the river, and a grinning fish performs some acrobatic jumps.

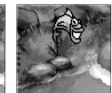

Timid Mouse
If the child clicks on the hole in the riverbank, a mouse appears and proceeds to wash herself, until she sees the viewer watching. Now bashful, she grabs her towel and runs back into her house.

FUN WITH NUMBERS

Some children love playing with numbers, but many find mathematics too difficult or just plain boring. Edutainment software can make learning math fun – or at least a lot less painful – by incorporating solid math practice work into a multimedia combination of animation, problem-solving exercises, learning games, and sometimes an adventure plot too. The majority of math edutainment titles also employ the perfect teachers – cartoon characters – who are friendly, patient, encouraging, and instantly forgiving.

I LOVE MATH
Dorling Kindersley's *I Love Math* presents traditional math problems in an imaginative adventure game. Players develop skills of arithmetic, geometry, and problem-solving as they try to revert the chaos caused by the mischievous Gretchen and Wilbur. A friendly canine, Old Bark, is always at hand to help.

ADVENTURES WITH MATH

Different multimedia titles teach math in very different ways. Some present activities that are no different from answering problems set by a teacher at a blackboard – but they are presented in a lively way by animated characters who offer encouragement and perform tricks, so the whole experience is made a lot more entertaining. Other titles present math as interactive games or puzzles that stretch the player's math skills to solve problems and win the game. And yet other titles weave math problems into animated adventures; because the problems are pivotal to the plot, the player has an added incentive to become involved in playing with numbers.

Time Machine
The game revolves around a time machine that transports players to four ancient worlds in need of their help. Every so often, they must engage in some rapid number crunching to restore its power supply.

Saving the World
In each of the ancient worlds, players use their math skills to restore harmony. In Atlantis, only an expert at fractions can successfully fix the plumbing.

Reaping the Reward
Success is rewarded with a series of animations. Making the right keys to unlock the Aztec temple will free the birds of paradise.

THE LOGICAL JOURNEY OF THE ZOOMBINIS

This classic adventure title from Broderbund develops children's awareness of mathematical concepts – such as set theory, algebra, graphs, organizing data – without them even realizing it. Each scene is introduced by an exuberant narrator who disguises all the hard work as fun and games.

Individual Characteristics
The Zoombinis have extremely unusual features that play a key part in solving many of the puzzles.

The Great Escape
The aim of the game is to help the Zoombinis escape to a new land, using a variety of skills to overcome the obstacles on the journey.

Developing Different Skills
Most scenes concentrate on one type of skill. In this scene, the child has to work out the correlation between the Zoombinis and Fleens, deciding how their features correspond to each other, and matching equivalent pairs.

Paying the Penalty
The child is encouraged to think accurately and swiftly by a system of penalties. Here, each extra guess results in a Zoombini being knocked off the branch and sent back to an earlier point.

Taking Action
In each scene the child has to work out a course of action. Here, that involves picking the Zoombinis that "match" the Fleens in the tree, then placing them on the hotspot to lure the Fleens down from the branch.

The Way Forward
The journey continues once the Zoombinis have lured their Fleen alter-egos away.

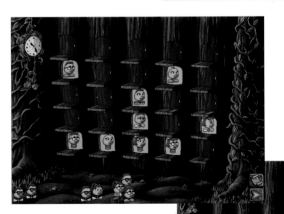

Looking for Clues
This scene is an exercise in pure logic. Each icon on the grid helps the child work out the set of conditions necessary to get each Zoombini safely across the ravine.

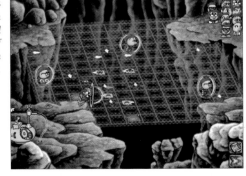

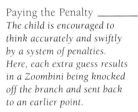

Levels of Difficulty
Each problem gets harder as the game progresses. Arranging the Zoombinis on a horizontal axis is relatively simple: considering the vertical axis too is more tricky.

Home
The game ends when all 625 Zoombinis have been safely escorted to Zoombiniton.

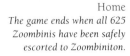

3-D ACTION GAMES

Yesterday's game was the platform game, in which you moved around a two-dimensional world. Today's games, however, have entered the third dimension. Multimedia machines are now powerful enough to produce realistic 3-D environments in which you can drive, fly, swim, kill, and die. Consoles have specialized graphics chips to handle these games, and many console buyers now choose machines purely on the basis of what they can run in 3-D. In fact, most console manufacturers become seriously concerned if they do not have a portfolio of major 3-D titles for their platform. Now that PCs have also become powerful enough to run 3-D games software, a serious hardware battle is being fought out on the field of 3-D combat.

3-D environments
For more on 3-D environments, see page 148

COMBAT GAMES

Among entertainment titles that have come to be regarded as classics, 3-D combat games such as *Doom* and *Quake* by id Software hold an unchallenged position. These games are often set in hostile underground labyrinths on distant planets or in vast space stations in imminent danger of being turned into a galaxy of neutrinos. With these complex settings, nonstop action, instant results, and sudden death around every corner, 3-D combat has taken the games market by storm, gaining devotees ranging from children as young as nine to middle-aged marketing directors. The core idea is essentially

DOOM DADDY
Few games have achieved the impact of *Doom* by id Software. The somber dark gray settings give a solid background to one of the more popular shoot-'em-ups.

simple – it amounts to little more than killing around corners, using awesome firepower. But it is this simplicity of action within complex and highly convincing settings that gives the games their unrivaled ability to involve the player. When you are moving fast through an unknown land, encountering aliens who are strangers to civilized conversation, there is neither the opportunity nor the need to sit back and think.

Simple but Convincing
The blocky graphics show how economically Tomb Raider's graphics have been drawn. Speed of movement compensates for the primitive drawing.

Martial Arts

The legendary *Doom* spawned a number of clones that developed variations on its settings, movement, weaponry, and player's opponents. However, another breed of game has emerged for people who prefer the intricacies and more contact-intensive rewards of martial arts action. Rather than having the perspective of the first-person gun, these games give you a figure that you manipulate, using the keyboard or joystick, to take on an opponent in weapon-free physical combat. The camera angle is controlled by the program: the camera appears to swoop and float around the action, taking whichever position shows the most mayhem.

A martial arts variation on 3-D combat is provided by *FX Fighter* from Argonaut/GTE. You select one fighter from eight cybermorphs and play against the program or another human player. The combat areas are varied, the animation is fast, the air is thick with flying kicks, and secret moves have to be found by rapid random moves of the joystick.

SKILLFUL PLAY
Each of the combatants in *FX Fighter* has unique skills that can be accessed by the player, using concealed key or joystick commands.

Camera Shots
The camera view changes, often to show the best angle for the player to select an attacking shot.

TOMB RAIDER
One of the most popular 3-D games to emerge recently is Core Design's *Tomb Raider*. Whereas *Doom* is set entirely in gloomy underground surroundings, *Tomb Raider* alternates elaborate buildings with outdoor, underwater, and historical settings. You take on the persona of Lara Croft, on a quest for adventure.

Offshore Antics
In this, the second game in the series, your adventure takes you to locations ranging from the Great Wall of China to an offshore oil rig.

Guns at the Ready
Beyond the doorway lies a room, but what danger lurks within?

Finding the Key
Success in Tomb Raider involves finding keys and other items – often in hazardous, heavily guarded areas – that will enable you to progress to the next stage of the game.

Third Person View
You control Lara from behind, but at any time you can assume her first person view, with the freedom to look all around you.

Animated Storylines
Noninteractive animations develop the plot, which you follow as you progress through the game.

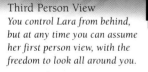

Heights and Depths
Tomb Raider *offers a greater variety of environments than many 3-D games, requiring you to master skills of climbing and swimming as well as shooting.*

Commandeered Transport
On your travels, you will encounter both abandoned and heavily guarded vehicles that you can drive. These form an integral part of the gameplay.

3-D FLYING AND DRIVING

Flying and driving titles make heavier demands on hardware than any other form of multimedia game. This is because they have a complex combination of essential requirements: high-speed movement; instant reaction to the player's control; and constant feedback so that the player can assess his or her degree of skill and success. In addition, because these games provide only one activity – flying or driving – they must add variety: a choice of cars or airplanes with different characteristics, and a number of different settings in which the action can take place.

INCREASING REALISM

Driving simulations first appeared on arcade machines in the 1970s, but their lack of processing power meant that the first games employed only two-dimensional graphics and sprites (small animated characters). The illusion of motion perspective was created by enlarging the sprites as they moved toward the edges of the screen.

The more powerful processors that appeared in the early 1980s enabled designers to use 3-D graphics for the first time. These early 3-D titles used wireframe shapes, where only the edges of the shapes were drawn, according to the rules of perspective. However, these shapes did at least allow the first flying simulations to be produced. These included the more complicated moves involved in flying an aircraft, such as climbing or descending to different altitudes and lateral airplane movements. The first simulations were set in outer space, filled with rudimentary planets, spacecraft, and missiles. When today's more powerful computers arrived, it became possible to simulate the experience of flying over a terrestial landscape.

MAGIC CARPET 2

The innovative *Magic Carpet 2*, by Bullfrog Productions, ignores airplanes in favor of a flying carpet. The convincing flying simulation places a great deal of control in the hands of the player, and the changes from fast-forward to hover to speedy retreat are smooth and instantaneous. You cannot crash, but the game is still not easy.

Hostile Worms
The worms in Magic Carpet 2 *have enormous segmented bodies that take a long time to come into view. Then they hurl fire balls at you.*

Balloon and Castle
When you kill a monster, its "life force" is transported to your castle by balloon for safekeeping. This life force gives you the power to cast spells.

Stinging Bees
These monsters sting if they can get close enough to you, but they do not die when they have struck – they live to sting again.

FLIGHT UNLIMITED

One of the outstanding features of *Flight Unlimited*, by Looking Glass Technologies, is the naturalistic appearance of the terrain as you fly over it. The landscape was created from digitized photographs, and as it unfolds below it can have a mesmerizing effect. The user can perform aerobatics – rolls and spins are simulated with a realism that some might find dizzying.

Surrounding Landscape
As you take off and climb over the hills beyond the airfield, this is your first sight of the surrounding countryside.

Grounded or Airborne
When starting a flying mission, you can decide whether the plane is stationary at the end of the runway, or airborne, or ready to taxi to the runway.

Landing the Airplane
Learning to line up the runway and land the airplane is not the least of the challenges that you will face.

FORMULA ONE GRAND PRIX 2

Microprose built on the success of the first version of its race game with this second release. A form of artificial intelligence determines how the different built-in race drivers respond to the changing conditions of the race – these drivers are based on the actual Formula One driver lineup.

Lifelike Models
The cars are realistically modeled on Formula One machines. They are texture-mapped and light-sourced for extra realism.

Changing Perspective
The game lends distance and perspective to its settings by graying out buildings as they recede into the background.

Grand Prix Manager
Microprose has also released a racing team manager game, Grand Prix Manager. The car setup can be customized in every detail, and the races take place on accurate representations of 16 race tracks from around the world.

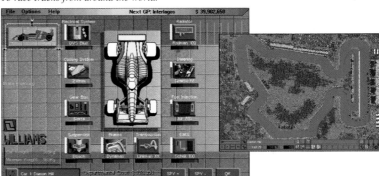

MULTIPLAYER GAMES

3-D action games have traditionally involved fighting your way past a series of monsters and enemies that the computer controls. But despite the amazing advances in artificial intelligence, many people are finding humans to be more challenging opponents and the trend for many new games is to concentrate on exciting multiplayer action. Although multiplayer games have been around for many years, they have only recently evolved beyond the text-based, role-playing games of the eighties. Advances in graphics and communications technologies have at last enabled multiplayer games played over a network to compete with the gameplay that a standalone computer can provide.

NETWORK GAMES

Multiplayer games have been around since the earliest computer games, but most of the early games that let players compete against one another were made for the dedicated games consoles or arcade machines. Few let players compete through two joysticks or by sharing a keyboard: more usually, multiplayer gaming simply meant taking turns against the computer and comparing scores at the end. Since character-based martial arts games emerged, arcade consoles have routinely supported player-against-player action, but serious multiplayer gaming is no longer the exclusive territory of the arcades. Now players can compete by using a cable to connect two powerful personal computers together, or a Local Area Network, common in most medium to large offices. Both methods offer a fast connection, but a network enables more than two players to join in, using computers that need not necessarily be in the same room. And since the advent of on-line gaming, opponents can even battle it out using computers located on opposite sides of the globe.

Games consoles
For more on games consoles, see page 92

Martial arts games
For more on martial arts games, see page 46

QUAKE II

Id Software's *Quake* was the first major game designed primarily for multiplayer action. *Quake II*, shown here, continues that trend, allowing up to 32 players to fight against each other simultaneously over a local network, or on-line via the Internet. As part of the package, Id Software provides a number of special servers to which users can connect if they want to play the game on-line.

ON-LINE GAMING

Many home computer users are unable to play network games because they do not have access to more than one computer. On-line games are played over the Internet, using a one-to-one modem connection with a friend, or by connecting via an Internet service provider to a special games network or server. Games networks provide a ready-made army of opponents, but the technical difficulties of sending data over the Internet do have some drawbacks: players may be affected by latency (the length of time data takes to reach its destination) and packet loss, both of which can slow down or interrupt gameplay. Still, as games designers produce better algorithms to overcome these problems, and as modems and computers get faster, they are becoming less of an issue.

Internet
For more on the Internet, see page 164

Packet loss
For more on packet loss, see page 164

Cooperative Play
Players can choose to fight cooperatively, in teams, in some cases with a mission to capture the enemy's flag. Here, Player 1 defends a team-mate from enemy attack.

Communicating
Players can communicate with one another by pressing a special key on their keyboard and then typing. Messages flash up on screen for all players to see.

Choosing a Skin

Teams of players can elect to wear their own custom-designed suits and masks, called skins. When competing side-by-side against other teams or individuals, skins help players to identify fellow team-members at a glance.

Individual Players

Players 3, 4, and 5 are competing as individuals. With no team members to defend them, they must shoot on sight.

Vantage Points

The complex settings and multilevel rooms offer a multitude of places to lurk in wait for enemy players.

INTERACTIVE MOVIES

The idea of directing and taking part in their own movie has instant appeal for most people. And, with interactive movies, multimedia has made this possible for the games player. An interactive movie involves the player on several levels: he or she can watch the movie unfold, and direct the sequence of events. The essential feature that makes this level of involvement possible is the use of video sequences showing actors playing roles in the game. The quality of an interactive movie will depend on how much video is included, the way it is used, and how much opportunity it provides for player input.

MAKING IT INTERACT

In an ideal world, the player of an interactive movie would be able to completely determine the movie's outcome; in practice, due to the limitations of space on a CD-ROM, players are presented with predetermined options. One approach is to provide the player with long sequences of video, and then allow him or her to choose from various courses of action until the solution to a problem is found, and the game can continue. These movies effectively have a single plot through which the player travels. A second technique is to use multiple plots. With this approach, the player's actions alter the flow of the storyline and the video that appears will depend on the choice the player has made. This makes for a more truly interactive movie.

The Great Outdoors
Not all of the action takes place inside the increasingly claustrophobic house: some key scenes happen outdoors.

The Daedalus Encounter

In this Mechadeus game, the player has two human accomplices on video, (one shown below). The player remotely controls an airborne probe to explore regions into which the actors are unable to go, and translates alien languages so that new areas can be opened up and vital controls operated.

Player's View
The interface consists of a set of controls notionally wired into the player's brain.

Moving Image
The video footage of Adrienne moving through the house is superimposed on rooms created using 3-D computer graphics.

Intercutting
Phantasmagoria uses many standard film-making techniques, including intercutting close-up shots in the footage to heighten elements of the drama.

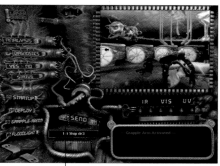

Logic Puzzle
The player encounters puzzles such as this one, where a logic circuit has to be set up by manipulating binary switches on color-coded components of the circuit.

PHANTASMAGORIA

These richly colored shots from Sierra's *Phantasmagoria* show the main setting for this interactive movie. Adrienne and Don have bought a vast rambling house that once belonged to an illusionist but has remained empty and undisturbed for years. The player directs Adrienne as she explores the house and its surroundings and slowly begins to discover its dark secrets. The title also includes noninteractive footage that contains important developments in the story.

Labyrinth
The main house is a labyrinth of stairs, passages, and rooms that each contain different surprises and clues.

Close-up Corner
The most significant parts of the house are shown in close-up and vivid detail.

Opening Doors
Some rooms require the imaginative use of found objects before they can be entered. Here, Adrienne is using a poker – found in the dining room – to open a trapdoor.

AWAITING DEVELOPMENTS

This complete game screen shows Adrienne waiting patiently to be given a direction to follow or an object to examine.

The Hint Keeper
Hints are available from an irascible crimson skull that watches your every move.

Pointer
The normal single yellow pointer turns red when moved over a "hot" object, or becomes an arrow to indicate a possible direction. Either can be chosen by clicking the mouse button.

Collecting Objects
An inventory stores found objects for later use; they can be viewed in rotating 3-D by moving them over the eyeball.

INTERACTIVE MUSIC

Interactive multimedia has opened up new avenues for artists, such as David Bowie, who are actively exploring it for themselves. Some music companies are using the potential of multimedia to provide enhanced CDs. These are CD-ROM versions of audio discs, which have an additional track containing both audio and multimedia information. As film companies, too, turn toward combining audio soundtracks and interactive content, enhanced CDs may soon become the most common recorded-music format in the home.

Enhanced CDs
For more on enhanced CDs, see page 81

MUSIC WITHOUT INSTRUMENTS

Most multimedia music CD-ROMs include interactive elements of some kind. Some titles simulate the experience of working in a recording studio, allowing you to mix your own tracks using a number of prerecorded samples or by adding your own recorded samples. Other titles promote the creative output of a musician or group – perhaps centered on a new album – by inviting you to explore a virtual world created from sound, images, and video clips relating to their life, work, and backlist. Some artists are now producing work specifically for multimedia.

ROCK 'N ROLL YOUR OWN
This title from The Learning Company presents eight prerecorded songs that can either be played as they were recorded or be remixed and saved to disk. *Rock 'n Roll Your Own* is not intended to replace "serious" musical sampling and sequencing software. It is more a tool kit introducing some of the concepts that lie behind the digital editing of music.

Record the Session
You can use this button to record and play back sessions you are especially pleased with.

Add Your Own Samples
Using a microphone and your computer's sound card, you can record new sounds or vocals and use them to enhance – or replace – elements of the songs provided.

Keyboard Sampling
A keyboard facility lets you construct your own tunes.

Using the Vib-a-tron
After choosing a sound from the Vib-a-tron's drop-down menu, you can add "scratch" effects to the sound by dragging the mouse back and forth over this area.

Watch a Video
Each song section is accompanied by a video clip.

Vocalizer
Click on these buttons at any time during playback to insert a vocal sample.

Control Screens
Each song has its own control screen. You can choose instrumental and vocal segments from this, combine them, and play them in sequence.

Songalizer
To choose the sequence in which your samples will be played, you need to drag the buttons (labeled I through X) from the left of the screen into the free spaces on the Songalizer.

MAJOR ROCK STARS ON CD-ROM

In BMG's *Jump, the David Bowie Interactive CD-ROM*, you explore a virtual world based on a skyscraper. By following the corridors, you find rooms containing material related to the *Black Tie, White Noise* album. Pointing and clicking your mouse reveals photographs, interviews, and video clips – including four music videos. You can also take an active role by editing an audio track and a video track, saving your favorite mixes to play back later.

Transport Controls

Video Screen

Edit Your Own Video
You can edit a master video by mixing video sequences from five different sources to accompany the audio playback. Clicking on a preview screen makes it appear in the main video screen. This sequence can be played back or saved to disk.

Track Sliders

Mix Your Own Track
You can mix your own version of the audio track Black Tie, White Noise by moving the track sliders to alter the volume of voices and instruments during playback.

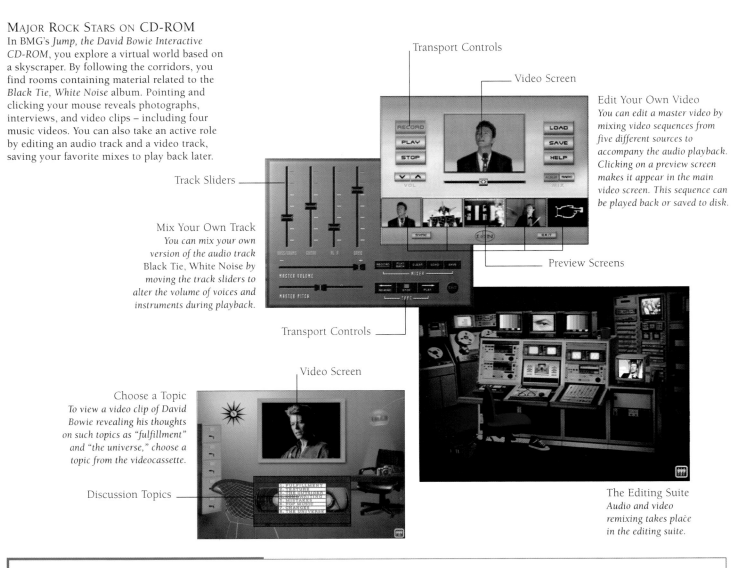

Transport Controls

Preview Screens

Video Screen

Choose a Topic
To view a video clip of David Bowie revealing his thoughts on such topics as "fulfillment" and "the universe," choose a topic from the videocassette.

Discussion Topics

The Editing Suite
Audio and video remixing takes place in the editing suite.

Audio CD and CD-ROM Combined

Sarah McLachlan, The Freedom Sessions is an eight-track audio CD from Arista with an additional multimedia track that can only be accessed when the CD is played on a computer. The multimedia track contains samples of more than 30 songs, speeches, photographs, and video clips promoting the work of the artist.

Trip to Thailand
Words, music, and video document a visit organized by the World Vision charity.

CD+MM
When this CD was produced in 1995, the makers described their title as CD+MM. They advised listeners to avoid track 1 (the multimedia track) when playing the CD on conventional audio equipment, since they would hear only static or silence. Later titles have avoided this problem.

Touring Scrapbook
This contains photographs and spoken descriptions of the tour venues on the map.

Today's multimedia computer is the product of several decades of extremely rapid advances in computer technology. This chapter looks inside a computer to show how the many components work – from mouse to monitor, from CD-ROM drive to speakers – and how they work together to bring multimedia from a compact disc to you.

INSIDE A PERSONAL COMPUTER

To ENJOY MULTIMEDIA IT IS NOT necessary to understand how computers work – but, as with any technology, it can be fascinating to find out what is going on. Examining the components of a multimedia computer provides an insight into the computer's role both in storing the images, sounds, and words of the real world in digital format, and in playing them back in the analog form we understand. As the world's most popular multimedia player, the IBM-compatible PC is shown here for illustration, but most processes also apply to other desktop computers. Information travels into the computer via a CD-ROM drive, keyboard, or mouse, and out via the screen or speakers. The processor, the "brain" of the computer, manages the overall flow of information both ways.

THE MULTIMEDIA PC
PCs consist of three main parts: input devices (such as a keyboard or mouse), output devices (such as a monitor), and the system unit, which houses the main electrical components. This cross section shows the system unit of a typical multimedia PC – that is, a PC that comes with a CD-ROM drive and sound facilities.

Expansion Slots
Expansion slots can be fitted with different expansion cards to add to a PC's capabilities.

Expansion Cards
Each expansion card consists of a fiberglass circuit board equipped with chips and other electronic components. An expansion card is used to add certain functions to a computer – for example, a sound card dramatically improves the PC's sound capabilities.

I/O PORTS
The Input/Output ports at the back of the computer facilitate the transfer of data into and out of the computer. Keyboards, printers, and modems are all examples of I/O devices. Most expansion cards have I/O ports on the back of the board.

Joystick Port
When playing games, it is often easier to control movements with a joystick than with a keyboard or a mouse.

Motherboard
This is where most of the electronic units of a computer reside; they are connected by metallic tracks printed on the motherboard.

Support Chips
The CPU is not the only processor on the motherboard.

Modem Port
By plugging in a device called a modem, a computer can use a telephone line to send and receive fax or voice messages, or connect to the Internet.

Sound Jacks
The jacks and the port on the back of the sound card are used for plugging in a microphone, speakers, or electronic instruments.

Bus
A bus is a network of metallic connectors that carries data, in the form of electrical pulses, from one component to another. A PC has several different types of buses.

THE BINARY SYSTEM

Computers store and manipulate all data and information – programs, pictures, and so on – in the form of numbers. These numbers are not ordinary decimal numbers; instead, the computer uses the binary system, which contains only two digits: 1 and 0 (somewhat like the dot and dash of Morse code). Each binary digit (1 or 0), known as a bit, is represented in the computer by alternative electrical states – an electrical current (on) represents the number 1, and no current (off) stands for 0. By stringing bits together, the computer can express any number as a sequence of electrical pulses. In computers, bits are usually grouped together in eights, and each group is known as a byte.

Hard Disk Drive
A hard disk is the computer's long-term memory. It is used for the storage of programs and data. Its capacity is measured in megabytes (a million bytes) or gigabytes (a thousand megabytes).

RAM (Random Access Memory)
RAM is the computer's main memory. It is used as a temporary storage area for all the programs that the computer is running.

CD-ROM Drive
The CD-ROM drive plays the data stored on CD-ROMs and audio CDs. Most drives only read data, but it is possible to get specialized drives that can also record data onto "recordable" CDs.

Sound waves
For more on digitizing sound, see page 123

Images
For more on digitizing images, see page 134

CPU (Central Processing Unit)
The CPU (or processor) does the actual computing and makes the whole computer work. It acts on program instructions, performs calculations, and controls the transfer of data along the bus.

Speakers
Some PCs have built-in speakers; others come with powerful external speakers that plug directly into the back of a sound card via an I/O port.

Counting in Binary

Binary is a counting system based on the two digits 1 and 0 (or on and off). On the right are the numbers one to five in binary – if you add up the value of the places marked with a 1, you can see how they add up to the decimal equivalent. So, for example, 0101 means no 8s + one 4 + no 2s + one 1, or 4+1, which equals 5 in decimal.

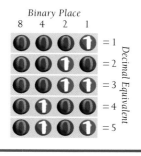

Binary Place
8 4 2 1

= 1
= 2
= 3
= 4
= 5

Decimal Equivalent

CODING AND FILING

Text is turned into binary code by assigning a specific number to each individual letter, and then representing that number in bits (for example, the capital letter A is given the number 65, and this is represented as 01000001 in binary). Numbers are represented in a different way to allow arithmetic operations to be carried out.

Sounds and pictures can be turned into numbers, and thus into binary code, using broadly similar methods. To digitize sound waves, the computer first divides them into thousands of tiny sections; then each section is measured for the strength of the signal at that point in time and the measurement is converted into a binary number. Images, too, are divided into parts – a grid of thousands of tiny colored dots – and then each dot is assigned a number that corresponds to its color.

Whatever type of information has been digitized, it can then be stored as a block of binary code on a storage medium such as a hard disk, floppy disk, or CD-ROM. This block of code is known as a file. As well as containing the numbers that represent the actual data, each file has additional coding to signify the name of the file, what type of information the numbers represent, and how the information is organized.

THE HARD FACTS ABOUT SOFTWARE

The key to understanding how computers work is knowing the difference between hardware and software. Hardware comprises all the internal and external elements that you can see and touch; software is a set of instructions that tells the hardware what to do and how to interact with the user. Software can be divided into two main categories: operating systems and programs.

OPERATING SYSTEMS

The operating system is the computer's master control software – it manages the keyboard, screen, and disk drives, and runs programs. When you switch on a computer, the operating system is automatically loaded into RAM (memory).

On the PC, the operating system is usually either Microsoft's Windows or IBM's OS/2. Like the Macintosh operating system, these examples of the picture-based GUI (Graphical User Interface) have made PCs much simpler to use than when commands were typed onto a blank screen.

GUI
For more on the Graphical User Interface, see page 85

MICROSOFT WINDOWS
As the most popular operating system in the world, Windows controls over 80 percent of the world's PCs.

SOFTWARE PROGRAMS
Computer programs range from productive tools such as Microsoft *Word* (below) to games on CD-ROM, such as Core Design's *Tomb Raider* (below right).

PROGRAMS

Programs can be classified in several ways. Some are used as productive tools (such as word processors), and are known as applications. Others (such as multimedia titles) are made for information and entertainment.

Programs are usually written for a specific operating system; for example, a CD-ROM title written for Microsoft Windows may not be understood by the Macintosh. Some programs are "dual-format" and will work on both Windows and Macintosh operating systems.

Programs are stored on a hard disk, a floppy disk, or a CD-ROM. When you use a program, some of its data is loaded into RAM, where it sits alongside the operating system. This gives the CPU (Central Processing Unit) fast and easy access to the data.

3-D Graphics Software

GRAPHICS COMPUTER
Powerful workstations such as this Silicon Graphics "Indy" computer are often dedicated to running specialized graphics software.

GEOMETRY ENGINE
The special graphics chips inside the Indy come on an expansion card, or "geometry engine." The card calculates the most common graphics functions, taking the load off the main processor.

Workstations

Multimedia titles (especially games) often contain exquisite graphics produced with specialized 3-D graphics programs that only work on a powerful breed of computer known as a workstation. Once created, these graphics can be displayed on a desktop computer.

Workstations were originally developed for graphical applications such as CAD (Computer-Aided Design). They contain special hardware that speeds up complex math calculations, and vast amounts of RAM. Many use a notoriously unfriendly operating system called Unix. Workstations are more powerful and more expensive than desktop computers, but as many high-end PC and Macintosh systems are now used for 3-D and video applications, the distinction between them is blurring.

THE PROCESSOR

The CPU, usually known simply as the processor, controls the computer and takes decisions based upon the information it receives. Modern processors, such as Intel's Pentium II, make about 200 million decisions a second, and most of the rest of the computer is dedicated to relaying information to and from the processor.

The processor receives two types of information: instructions and data. The instructions come from programs and consist of orders such as "add these figures together." The data are the binary numbers, text, pictures, or sound; the processor interprets these and moves them about the computer.

The processor receives instructions from the program in RAM; it also uses RAM as a sort of "scratchpad" on which to perform calculations.

RAM CHIPS AND PROCESSOR

A computer's performance is governed by the speed of its processor and the amount of RAM it has. Both can usually be "upgraded" – in the case of RAM, by slotting more chips in, and in the case of the processor, by replacing it with a newer, more powerful chip.

Brainy Chip
The processor chip is the true brain of the computer.

Processor
To handle the amount of information involved in playing animated sequences, video clips, and sound tracks, a multimedia computer requires a fast and powerful processor.

RAM Chips
The computer's primary memory, RAM, consists of rows of chips that serve as a temporary storage area for the operating system and any programs that are running.

Heat Sink
The latest processors operate at such high speeds that they can overheat. A heat sink helps to cool the processor down – some heat sinks even have built-in fans.

Upgrade Socket
Many PCs come with a processor upgrade socket on the motherboard. When a new, more powerful processor is manufactured, it can be fitted into this socket to replace the existing one.

Lever
The small lever arm makes it easy to remove the processor chip when upgrading.

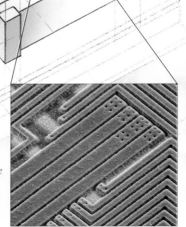

Inside a Processor Chip
This magnified section of the inside of a processor chip shows the integrated circuits imprinted on its surface. The circuits carry the electrical currents that make up the on/off pulses of binary code.

MORE AND MORE BITS

Like everything else in the computer, the processor deals with binary data. The instructions and data it receives are just a sequence of bits, and the number of bits it can handle at once allows its performance to be measured.

Each new generation of processors is marked by a huge leap in processing power. The 8088 in the first IBM PC was 8-bit, which meant that it could manipulate only one byte of information at a time. The next generation of processor, the 80286, was 16-bit, and the latest, the Pentium, is 64-bit. In a little more than a decade, data processing abilities have increased eightfold.

CLOCK SPEED

Data handling is only one aspect of processor performance, however. The clock speed, quoted in MHz (megahertz), units of frequency, is a measurement of how quickly the processor can act on an instruction.

If you think of one hertz as being equivalent to one clock tick, then one megahertz equals one million ticks per second. Early PCs ran at about 5 MHz – that is, they could process about five million instructions per second. An average PC these days runs at about 200 to 300 MHz, but manufacturers are already developing processors with speeds of over 500 MHz.

FROM MOUSE TO MONITOR

Multimedia computers receive their instructions and data from software stored on a disk or CD-ROM. But software does not act on its own – it requires input from the user, via an input device such as a mouse or a keyboard. When the processor has followed the software instructions and processed the multimedia data, it also needs some means of presenting the output – a monitor and speakers. Here we follow the passage of data from mouse to monitor.

MOUSE MOVES

When you use multimedia software and you want to access a point on the screen – a hotspot, for example – you move the mouse across a flat surface until the pointer is at the desired position and click the mouse button. As you move the mouse, the ball on its underside drives two rollers. Via the mouse cable, these rollers send information about the movement of the mouse to the processor, so that it always knows where to position the mouse pointer on screen.

Hotspot
For more on hotspots, see page 19

PLUG-AND-PLAY

The processor uses a part of the operating system called the mouse driver to interpret the signals from the mouse. Similarly, the keyboard, screen, sound card, and CD-ROM drive all have their own driver software.

To add a new device to a PC, the owner has to install its driver software. Before the introduction of modern operating systems, this task was often fraught with difficulty, as the settings for the new driver frequently clashed with those of an existing one.

The latest operating systems have "plug-and-play" capabilities. This means that the computer can determine the configuration needed to make a new device work, and automatically install any required drivers from the disks supplied with the hardware.

THE MOUSE
With its "point and click" action, the mouse is ideally suited to multimedia software. These days most CD-ROM titles require a mouse, although an alternative input device, the joystick, is often used for games.

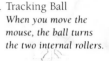

Tracking Ball
When you move the mouse, the ball turns the two internal rollers.

Horizontal Roller
This roller picks up the side-to-side movements of the mouse.

Button
Clicking a mouse button sends a signal to the processor, which alerts the program to the action.

Vertical Roller
This roller picks up the backward and forward movements of the mouse.

Processing Circuitry
This transmits the roller movements to the computer, as a series of binary codes.

The Computing Process

Computing tasks involve a complex set of operations, most of which are controlled and monitored by the processor. Here you can follow, in simplified form, the journey data takes from input to output. The following pages describe the process in more detail.

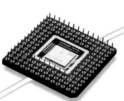

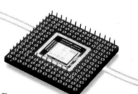

MOUSE
When you click the mouse button to initiate an action (for example, starting a video sequence), a signal is sent to the processor.

PROCESSOR
The processor sends a message to the program, indicating the area of screen where the action was performed.

PROGRAM
The processor checks through the instructions of the program stored in RAM (memory) to see what action should be taken in response. In this example it discovers that a particular video clip must be launched.

PROCESSOR
The processor sends a request for the relevant video file to the CD-ROM.

BUS OPERATIONS

The bus is the network of thin metallic tracks that transports data around the motherboard of the computer. There are a number of different buses inside a PC. For a start, three separate buses connect the processor to the rest of the computer – the data bus, the address bus, and the control bus, collectively known as the system bus.

THE EXPANSION BUS

Another type of bus is the expansion bus, which connects expansion cards, such as sound cards, to the motherboard of the computer. The size, or "width," of the bus is measured in bits, and is critical to multimedia because it determines the speed at which sound and graphics are delivered.

The expansion bus in early PCs was 8-bit and matched the capacity of the processor. When processor capacity went up to 16-bit, so did the data bus. To avoid making all the 8-bit cards redundant, however, the bus was redesigned to take both 8- and 16-bit cards. This system is known as ISA (Industry Standard Architecture). Even though ISA increased the capacity of the bus, it did not alter its speed, which remained at a slow 8-10 MHz.

Integrated Circuit

Data Bus
The data bus carries data between the disk drives, processor, and RAM.

Address Bus
The address bus carries information about where in RAM (memory) the data is going to or coming from.

Control Bus
The control bus is used to signal the direction of the flow of data.

THE SYSTEM BUS
This illustration shows the three buses that make up the system bus. In reality all bus tracks look identical – they have been colored here to highlight the difference.

EXPANSION SLOTS
The connectors of an expansion card fit into an expansion slot. An expansion slot is just an extension of the system bus. Most PCs made today have a mixture of PCI and ISA slots to maintain compatibility with old expansion cards.

PCI Expansion Slots
PCI expansion slots can carry 32 or 64 bits of data at a time, at high speeds.

Original 8-bit Expansion Slot

ISA Extension
An extension was added to make it a 16-bit slot.

THE PCI LOCAL BUS
The ISA bus was fine for 16-bit processors, but when 32- and 64-bit processors arrived, it held up data between the processor and expansion cards. Its narrow width and slow speed meant that it was unable to process data as quickly as it received it, and the processor was constantly having to wait for data that was held up by the bus.

PCI (Peripheral Component Interconnect) local buses changed all that by allowing peripheral components, such as expansion cards and printers, to communicate with each other directly – 64 bits at a time, and at high speed. The result of using PCI local buses is that multimedia titles run much faster and with fewer pauses.

CD-ROM
When the video clip is located on the CD-ROM, its data is delivered into RAM.

OPERATING SYSTEM
The processor follows instructions in the operating system stored in RAM to identify the data as it is delivered, separating graphics from sound. It then sends the data to the graphics and sound cards.

GRAPHICS/SOUND CARD
The graphics and sound cards change the received data from digital to analog and output the result.

SCREEN AND SPEAKERS
The monitor displays the video clip, and the speakers play the sound.

THE CD-ROM

A very simple idea led to the invention of the CD-ROM – it was to store computer data instead of sound on a CD. The disc itself consists of a wafer-thin aluminum layer sandwiched between two protective layers of plastic. During manufacture, data is stamped into the disc in the form of pits (hollow areas) and lands (flat areas), which represent the 1s and 0s of binary data. The pits and lands form a spiral running from the center of the disc to its edge.

Manufacture
For more on how CD-ROMs are made, see page 81

REFLECTED LIGHT

During playback, a read head containing a laser beam is passed over the spinning CD-ROM via a system of prisms and mirrors. The beam passes through the plastic coating to the aluminum layer. Most of the beam is absorbed when it hits a pit, so that only a little light is reflected. When a land is encountered, most of the light is bounced back.

The reflected light is directed back – again, via a prism – to a light-sensitive photo diode, which translates the light patterns back into binary data.

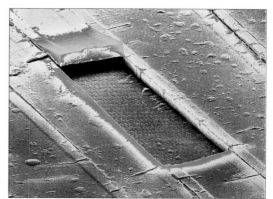

PITS AND LANDS
This image (magnified over 250 times) shows the plastic coating of a CD peeled back to reveal the aluminum layer with its lands and pits.

INSIDE A CD-ROM PLAYER
CD-ROM players contain finely tuned components that direct a laser beam onto the disc and back again. All that touches the disc surface is light, so discs do not deteriorate when played.

5 Variable Rotation
The disc rotates to bring new data in front of the laser. To keep the rate at which data is accessed constant, the disc rotates more slowly when the read head is nearer the center.

6 Return Journey
The light is reflected by the surface of the disc and returns through the read head, the mirror, and the prisms. On the return journey, the prisms redirect the beam to the photo diode.

4 Read Head
The read head moves across the radius of the disc, directing the laser beam to the relevant area.

3 Mirror
The mirror redirects the incoming light to the read head.

2 Prisms
The laser beam passes through a system of prisms that refine the beam.

SPEED RESTRICTIONS

While no one doubts that CD-ROM is a revolutionary technology, finding and transferring data at speed is not one of its outstanding features. Computers need to access chunks of data that are stored on various parts of a disc, and with CD-ROM it can take a long time for the laser head to move across the disc and reach the relevant data.

The amount of time it takes the laser head to locate data on the disc is known as the seek time. A typical CD-ROM drive has a seek time of about 150 milliseconds – about 20 times more than the seek time of a fast hard disk. This appears to be the physical limit for present CD-ROM technology.

DATA DIFFICULTIES
Compared with hard disks, CD-ROM drives are slow at transferring data from the disc to the processor. This is especially noticeable with video, which often looks jerky, or can only be displayed in a tiny window.

Video compression
For more on video compression, see page 156

⑦ Photo Diode
This light-sensitive component translates the light reflected back from the disc into binary code and then passes it on to the processor.

① Laser Diode
This produces a highly accurate laser beam that can be targeted to within 1/25,000th of an inch (0.001 mm).

DATA TRANSFER RATES

Speed considerations do not end with seek times – the data must still be transferred from the disc to the PC's memory at an acceptable speed. This is known as the data transfer rate.

Early CD-ROM drives transferred data at 150 Kb/s (kilobytes per second). These drives are now virtually extinct, and most computer owners now have at least a double-speed drive with a data transfer rate of 300 Kb/s. Recent purchasers probably have drives of eight-speed or higher; these transfer data at a rate of 1,200 Kb/s.

Despite the steady increase in data transfer rates (24-speed drives are available), CD-ROM drives are still about ten times slower at transferring data than an average hard disk. The struggle to get data to the screen becomes especially apparent with video, although new video compression techniques have reduced the amount of data needed to produce good-quality, full-screen video sequences.

DVD DRIVE
DVD drives, such as this one from Sony, can offer access to as much as 17 Gb of data at a time. They have fast seek times and data-transfer rates, and can greatly improve the playback quality of multimedia.

DIGITAL VIDEO DISC

Although CD-ROM drives have become much faster since they first appeared in the late 1980s, the storage capacity of a CD has not changed at all. This remains at a stable 650 Mb (megabytes). In 1997, however, a new high-density disc called DVD (digital video disc) arrived to challenge the future of the traditional compact disc.

DVD technology was developed jointly by Sony and Philips. It features a dramatic increase in the number of pits and lands on a disc, coupled with an improved mechanism for focusing the laser beam. These improvements make it possible to store two layers of data on one side of a DVD, and to use both sides of the disc. A dual-layer, double-sided DVD can hold up to 17 Gb (17,000 Mb) of data – enough to store over eight hours of digital video with multiple-channel sound.

Today, the CD-ROM is still the multimedia industry standard, but as DVD drives become widespread, perhaps by the turn of the century, DVD may replace the CD completely. The only other method of accessing more than the standard 650 Mb is to use a CD-ROM stack system.

THE MONITOR

The display area of a monitor is divided into a grid of pixels (short for picture elements). Every pixel is made up of three tiny dots of phosphor (a substance that glows when stimulated by electrons); one dot is red, one green, and one blue. By varying the brightness of each dot, electron beams within the monitor can make any pixel produce any color – and by combining patterns of pixels, on-screen graphics are made. Not all displays are equal, however. The resolution (sharpness) of the picture, measured as the number of pixels across by the number of pixels down, depends on the monitor and the graphics card that runs it. So does the number of different colors each pixel can display – the color depth – which ranges from two (black and white) to 16 million (photo-quality color).

Graphics
For more on graphics, see page 130

THE GRAPHICS CARD

The CPU (processor) is constantly working out digital maps of what should appear on the screen – it delegates the task of actually displaying them to the graphics card, which has its own set of processors. The CPU sends each new map to the video cache, an area of temporary memory on the card.

The graphics controller chip on the card reads the maps as they arrive in the buffer, and changes them into analog signals – patterns of varying voltages. These voltages power three electron beams at the back of the monitor, which give each pixel on the screen the right mix of red, green, and blue to make the required color.

GRAPHICS CARD
The processor calculates what should appear on the screen – the graphics card converts it from a digital signal into an analog one for the monitor.

Graphics Controller

Video Cache

INSIDE THE MONITOR
The monitor turns patterns of voltages from the graphics card into the patterns of light that make up the final image on the screen. Inside the monitor, beams of electrons are cleverly controlled to color every point on the screen.

1) Electron Beams
Three guns fire electrons at the screen. The strength of each beam is controlled by the incoming signal from the graphics card.

2) Shadow Mask
This thin sheet of metal has tiny holes so arranged that as one beam passes through, it hits only red pixel dots at the front of the screen, the second hits only green, and the third only blue.

3) Path of Electron Beams
The beams sweep left to right across the screen, one row at a time. The entire screen is scanned at least 60 times a second.

4) Grid of Pixels
A closer look at the screen shows the gridlike pattern of pixels that makes up the picture. An average monitor "colors in" up to 750,000 pixels to draw each image on the screen.

5) Pixels in Close-up
A pixel is a group of three colored dots of phosphor, which glow when the electron beams hit them. Different colors are produced by varying the strength of each beam.

SOUND SYSTEM

Without a sound card, the PC has slightly less of a voice than the trashcan-sized robot R2D2 from the movie *Star Wars*. The sound card became the first essential multimedia add-on when CD-ROM drives were still an expensive luxury. Today's sound cards offer sophisticated, CD-quality music, speech, and sound effects.

Recording sound
For more on recording sound, see page 124

A sound card has two basic purposes. The first is recording sound – taking analog sound signals from a microphone, or music from an electronic instrument, and converting them into digital sound files. The second is playing back the digital sound files stored on a computer's hard disk or CD-ROM as analog sound, through headphones, speakers, or even a surround-sound stereo system.

TWO MACHINES IN ONE

There are two types of sound files that can be stored on a computer, and each one is dealt with by a different chip on the sound card.

Digital sound
For more on digital sound, see page 123

Digital sound files – digitized samples of real sounds – are played by a sampler chip, which changes them into an analog signal that can be played through speakers.

MIDI
For more on MIDI, see page 128

Also on the card is a synthesizer chip that deals with MIDI (Musical Instrument Digital Interface) files. MIDI files hold information similar to the notes in sheet music – "play B-flat using a piano voice," for example. To make MIDI music, the synthesizer chip follows the score, creating each note by manipulating the frequency of sine waves. If a sound card has a "wavetable" (a bank of digitized samples of real instruments), the synthesizer chip can produce more realistic music by basing each note on a real sound.

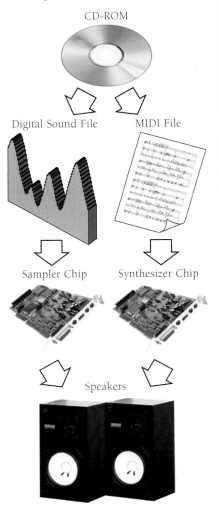

From CD to Speaker

To create sound for multimedia, a sound card converts CD-ROM sound files (which may be digital sound or MIDI) into signals for the speakers, as shown here.

CD-ROM

Digital Sound File   MIDI File

Sampler Chip   Synthesizer Chip

Speakers

SOUND CARD
One of the sound card's jobs is to play back sound from a disk or a CD-ROM. It does this by converting digital and MIDI sound data into the traditional analog sound signals of headphones and speakers.

Sampler Chip
This chip changes digital sound data into analog sound signals for playback, and vice versa.

Amplifier
A small amplifier boosts the analog signal so it is loud enough for headphones or small speakers.

Synthesizer Chip
This chip changes MIDI music files into the synthesized sounds of musical instruments.

Speaker Out
The amplified signal is fed to headphones or powered speakers, which turn it into sound waves we can hear.

Expansion Slot Connectors
The sound card plugs straight into an expansion slot on the PC motherboard.

MIDI/Joystick Port
The sound card can record and output sound through an electronic keyboard or drum machine. Games players can also use this socket to connect a joystick.

Multimedia is made possible by the machines that play it and made better by advances in computer technology. This chapter traces the story of home multimedia players – desktop computers and home consoles – and looks at the major players of each kind. It goes on to explore the heightened realism and interactivity offered by virtual reality machines.

PLATFORMS AND PLAYERS

THE STORY OF MULTIMEDIA IS THE story of the machines that make multimedia happen. It was the ever-increasing pace of progress in computer technology during the last two decades coupled with the huge growth in popularity of desktop computing and digital entertainment that made multimedia possible. For software developers, keeping up with the machines is a frenetic race against time – making quality titles for today's machines before tomorrow's devices arrive. For the machine makers, the battle is to produce tomorrow's hardware today, or at least before their rivals do. For the rest of us, the result is a vast and sometimes bewildering selection of multimedia players, or platforms, and the many different types of CDs and other storage media that can be used with them.

THREE KINDS OF MACHINES

It is not surprising that, on average, one multimedia title in three is returned to the store because the software does not match the owner's hardware. There are dozens of multimedia platforms, but essentially they come in three varieties. The first of these, the personal computers, are the direct descendants of the room-sized valve monsters of the 1940s. No longer the drab workhorses they once were, computers can offer dazzling multimedia performance.

By far the most popular multimedia machines, however, are the consoles – home entertainment systems that plug right into a television set. Because the console market is worth billions of dollars every year, the competition between manufacturers is extremely fierce. Most consoles are dedicated games machines, but some offer a range of educational and reference titles – these machines tend to be called simply "multimedia players" to avoid the games-only tag.

The third type of multimedia player is the virtual reality machine, which brings a high degree of realism and new kinds of interaction to multimedia entertainment. The leading edge of virtual reality, however, is in its serious applications – in architecture, industry, medicine, and the armed forces – where the high-tech equipment in use points toward the future of multimedia machines.

Personal computers
For more on personal computers, see page 84

Consoles
For more on consoles, see page 92

Virtual reality
For more on virtual reality, see page 102

Console
Home consoles play multimedia through a television set.

Desktop Computer
Equipped with a CD-ROM drive and sound hardware, a desktop computer becomes an advanced multimedia player.

Virtual Reality Machine
The expensive machines of the digital entertainment industry, such as this virtual reality machine, offer a new type of multimedia experience.

PHOTO CD
The Photo CD is a format designed by Kodak to hold high-quality photographic images only. Few players can use Photo CDs.

AUDIO CD
The original compact disc was invented to hold over 75 minutes of digital music. Most multimedia players can play audio CDs.

CD FORMATS

While the sophisticated machines of the amusement arcades have their software built in, multimedia for computers and most consoles comes on a compact disc (some consoles use cartridges). Multimedia CDs are physically the same as audio CDs but the information they carry is different. With the exception of the CD-i player, which has its own disc format – CD-interactive – most multimedia players use CD-ROM (Compact Disc Read-Only Memory). But the others may as well have their own formats, because although a CD-ROM drive can read any CD-ROM, each player uses different computer software.

CD-ROM drive
For more on CD-ROM drives, see page 74

VIDEO CD
A Video CD can store up to 74 minutes of full-screen video – a feature-length movie has to be split over two discs. Multimedia machines usually need extra hardware to play Video CDs.

CROSS-PLATFORM MULTIMEDIA
Some types of CDs can be used on a range of machines, but they do not offer full multimedia. Besides the original audio CD there are two other single-medium formats – Photo CD and Video CD. There is also a hybrid format – enhanced CD – which is a cross between a CD and a CD-ROM.

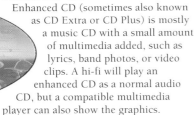

ENHANCED CD
Enhanced CD (sometimes also known as CD Extra or CD Plus) is mostly a music CD with a small amount of multimedia added, such as lyrics, band photos, or video clips. A hi-fi will play an enhanced CD as a normal audio CD, but a compatible multimedia player can also show the graphics.

CD-ROM AND CD-I
Both the CD-ROM and Philips' own-brand multimedia disc, the CD-i, can store sound, text, still and moving pictures, and computer software.

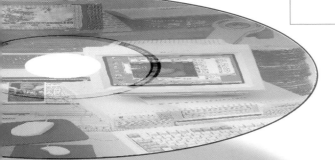

How a CD Is Made
Every type of CD is made in the same way. First, the digital data is fed to a laser, which burns the data into the photographic coating of a spinning glass disc. Next, the glass master is dipped in acid to etch the data in, and then a metal imprint is made. On the production line, the imprint is used to stamp heated plastic blanks. The pressed discs are coated with a layer of reflective aluminum, which takes the shape of the stamped data. Then each disc is given a protective lacquer coating to make the final CD.

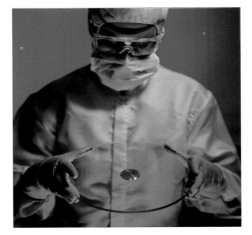

CHECKING THE GLASS MASTER
Because one speck of dust can ruin a CD, the master disc is handled in conditions that are hundreds of times cleaner than in an operating room.

DVD
Digital video disc is a high-density format that can store over 14 times as much data as CD-ROM. Over the next few years, DVD may begin to replace today's many CD formats, ushering in new audio, video, and multimedia formats of its own.

THE COMPUTER STORY

THE EARLIEST PROGRAMMABLE computer was conceived by Charles Babbage, an English mathematician (1792–1871). Babbage hit on the idea while building a mechanical calculating machine called the Difference Engine (inset). As this was 1823, the technology of the time did not allow his plans for a computer to bear fruit, but the ideas behind it – a device that would perform a variety of calculations according to a program that was input using punch cards – embodied many of the principles later used in the design of modern computers.

EARLY HISTORY

It was not until the invention of the vacuum tube in 1904 that the elements for building an electronic computer became available.

The vacuum tube, made of glass, encases a filament that produces electrons (subatomic particles that carry electricity) when heated. Depending on its construction, a vacuum tube can act as an amplifier, a signal detector, or a simple on/off switch. In early computers vacuum tubes were used mostly as amplifiers, but by about 1940 their function as on/off switches was used to represent binary code, with off standing for 0 and on standing for 1. Data was input via punch cards, and the various parts of the system had to be connected manually by cable, one at a time, as they were required.

Programming them was excruciatingly slow – a program that took five minutes to run could take several days to set up.

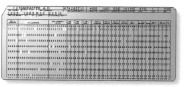

PUNCH CARDS
Data was fed into early vacuum tube computers via sheets of cardboard punched with holes.

Binary code
For more on binary code, see page 69

VACUUM TUBES TO TRANSISTORS

These early computers were used primarily by the military. World War II caused a spurt of innovation, and when the war ended, government departments began finding additional uses for the computer.

Vacuum-tube computers had many drawbacks, however. They were large, because vacuum tubes are bulky glass devices. They were unreliable, because the heating filaments could "blow," and the filaments also made the computers very hot. They were also limited in processing power, because the number of tubes that could reliably be used together was small.

These problems were solved in 1947, when Bell Telephone Laboratories in the United States invented the transistor. Transistors do the same things as vacuum tubes, but they use a small lump of a semi-conducting material such as silicon to act as an on/off switch.

1940s

VACUUM TUBES
Vacuum tubes were the first electronic components. They were used initially in radios to amplify the received signal, but by the early 1940s their ability to transfer or block electric current was being exploited to represent binary code in computers.

1946

ENIAC COMPUTER
The ENIAC (Electronic Numerical Integrator and Computer) was a war baby, created to solve problems with ballistics during World War II. It was really a giant calculator, since it could not store programs or data. Although it was finished too late to help with the war effort, the 30-ton machine remained in use by the US army for many years.

1950s

TRANSISTORS
When vacuum tubes in computers were replaced by transistors in the early 1950s, computers became smaller and cheaper. A transistor consists of a pinhead-sized piece of semiconducting material enclosed in a metal case about half an inch (12 mm) long.

MAINFRAME COMPUTERS

With small, reliable, cool-running transistors replacing vacuum tubes, computers became smaller, more powerful, and much cheaper. The new machines (known as mainframe computers) found their niche in large corporations such as banks, where their processing power – roughly equivalent to that of an average modern PC – was shared by many users at the same time.

By today's standards, mainframes were huge, sometimes filling several rooms. Programs were usually input using punch cards, and data was stored on reels of magnetic tape (the equivalent of today's hard disk drives).

By the start of the 1960s the familiar names of the mainframe computer world – such as IBM (International Business Machines) and Sperry Univac – controlled the computer market worldwide.

MAGNETIC TAPE
Transistor computers used plastic tape coated with metal to store data in the form of magnetic fields.

DOWN TO CHIP LEVEL

In 1959, an American firm named Texas Instruments showed that it was possible to etch multiple transistors on one piece of silicon using photographic techniques. The transistors could then be connected by metal tracks etched into the silicon. This arrangement became known as an integrated circuit, or silicon chip, and from this moment on technology moved inexorably toward cramming the maximum number of transistors into the minimum area of silicon.

In 1971, an integrated circuit manufacturer named Intel was asked to supply all the main components of a computer on one integrated circuit for a new electronic calculator being designed by a Japanese company. The result, the 4004 chip, was billed by Intel as a "computer on a chip." It was about the size of a baby's fingernail.

The 4004 was the world's first microprocessor. Its invention set the stage for the arrival of the microcomputer – which, after all, is essentially a calculator with improved processing power and a few extra parts.

Microprocessor
For more on processors, see page 71

THE SILICON CHIP
The chips you see inside a computer are built up in layers; each layer is drawn onto a sheet of transparent film that is miniaturized before its patterns are photographically etched onto a thin slice of silicon.

Transistor

Circuit Plan of One Layer

Transparency

1960s

MAINFRAMES
During the 1960s, mainframe computers were common in the scientific and business communities. Companies such as IBM, the best-known supplier of mainframes (such as that shown here, belonging to the System/360 series), introduced the concept of compatibility – all the members of this series could run the same software programs.

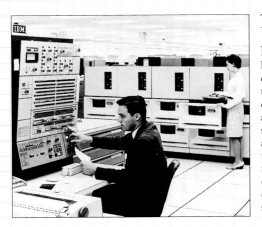

1971

MICROPROCESSORS
The personal computer revolution began with the invention of an integrated circuit known as a microprocessor. This "computer on a chip" is encased in a ceramic or plastic capsule for protection. A set of metal pins sticking out of the capsule connects the chip to the rest of the computer.

Ceramic Capsule

Microprocessor Chip

THE IBM PC

By 1980, there were over 200 brands of desktop computers in the United States alone. Wary of losing its position in the business market, mainframe manufacturer IBM began designing a PC.

The IBM personal computer was launched in 1981, less than a year after its inception. Built around Intel's new 8088 processor, the PC was twice as fast as its rivals. It also offered expansion slots for the addition of devices such as hard disks and extra memory.

Expansion slots
For more on
expansion slots,
see page 73

MICROSOFT'S BIG BREAK

The new processor could not run the standard CP/M as its operating system, so IBM asked a Seattle-based software house, Microsoft, to make a new CP/M-type program for the PC. Microsoft named the new operating system MS-DOS (for Microsoft Disk Operating System). For a number of years, MS-DOS was the dominant PC operating system, and its position has only recently been usurped by Windows (a more recent Microsoft system).

EMPIRE BUILDER
Microsoft cofounder Bill Gates was a billionaire by the age of 30, thanks to a contract to supply the IBM PC's operating system.

Although MS-DOS was similar to CP/M, it could not run CP/M software, so few applications were available for the IBM PC at its launch. In theory, this should have ensured the machine's failure; in practice, it was a huge success. Corporate America saw the IBM logo as a guarantee of quality and the PC (with MS-DOS) was soon setting the standards in personal computing.

MS-DOS
MS-DOS was controlled by typing in cryptic commands at the keyboard – this did nothing to endear it to beginners.

THE APPLE MACINTOSH

Anxious to keep the IBM PC at bay, Apple's next project found inspiration in the designs developed at Xerox PARC. Steve Jobs had visited the research center in 1979, returning to Apple with a head full of ideas (and a handful of Xerox employees).

Putting PARC's theories into practice would require a fast processor, and Apple's eye fell on the Motorola 68000. This chip processed data more efficiently than the Intel 8088 chip found inside the IBM PC, and it formed the basis of two new Apple machines, the Lisa and the Macintosh.

The Lisa arrived on the market in 1983, introducing the icons, menus, and mouse of Xerox PARC's GUI (Graphical User Interface) technology to the mass market, but to no avail. The job of displaying graphics on screen made the Lisa much slower than the PC, yet at $10,000 it cost almost twice as much. Computer buyers remained indifferent to its charms.

The Macintosh was launched one year later. Despite an enthusiastic reception from the press, it seemed destined to follow the Lisa into obscurity, when a couple of factors conspired to keep it alive. The first was the launch of Microsoft *Excel* for the Macintosh, which rapidly became the most popular spreadsheet program of the time. The other factor was the release of a number of "desktop publishing" applications, which turned the Macintosh into a one-stop graphics and printing shop.

Microsoft *Excel*
This spreadsheet program was hugely popular. Many people bought the Macintosh just for this program.

Monochrome Monitor
· *The IBM PC displayed green text on a black background, but a color graphics card could be slotted into an expansion slot to give extra colors.*

1981

ORIGINAL IBM PC

IBM launched two versions of its PC. The basic model came without a monitor and required a cassette player for data storage. The better model cost just over $4,300 and included a monitor, keyboard, and twin floppy disk drives.

Speaker
The PC offered a built-in loudspeaker that could do little more than bleep.

Floppy Disk Drives
Each of the two floppy disk drives could accommodate 160 Kb (kilobytes) of data.

1984

FIRST APPLE MACINTOSH

The Macintosh was launched with a single floppy disk drive, tiny built-in monochrome monitor, and no expansion slots. Compared to the IBM PC it was less powerful but easier to use because of its GUI. Software developers used the GUI to dramatic effect, and when Aldus Corporation created *PageMaker* (a graphic design program for laying out pages of magazines and books), the Macintosh found a role that no other computer could play.

MULTIMEDIA MOVES IN

Throughout the 1980s, personal computers grew and developed. IBM's PC was cloned (copied) by hundreds of manufacturers, and add-on hardware such as sound cards began appearing, extending the PC's capabilities. The Macintosh was redesigned to accommodate color graphics. A new system of storing digital data – the compact disc – arrived. And every few years, a new generation of microprocessor chips came along that doubled computing power.

When Intel introduced the 80386 chip in 1985, PCs finally received the power required to shift large amounts of sound and graphics around. Still, it was only in 1990 that multimedia software for the PC really took off, with the release of version 3.0 of Microsoft's Windows operating system.

Windows 3.0 introduced a standard method by which programs could communicate with multimedia hardware such as sound cards. Software manufacturers could now be assured that their products would work on any PC running Windows. As a result, the market in multimedia software took a giant leap forward. Subsequent versions of Windows have further enhanced the PC's capacity to handle multimedia by adding "plug-and-play" features for installing new hardware, such as graphics accelerator cards, support for the new generation compact disc, DVD, as well as integrated features for receiving multimedia on-line.

Sound cards
For more on sound cards, see page 77

MULTIMEDIA TITLES
CD-ROM-based software titles for the home, such as Microsoft's *Musical Instruments*, first appeared in the early nineties.

DVD
For more on DVD, see page 75

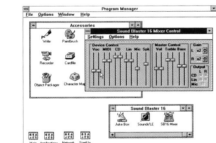

PROCESSING ADVANCES

As software grows more sophisticated, processor technology is evolving to meet its demands.

PCs and Macs have traditionally been built around a family of processors made by specific chip designers – Intel's 80000 line for the PC (such as the 80386 and 80486) and Motorola's 68000 series for the Mac.

Although they are different, both chip families are based on a technology known as CISC (pronounced "sisk"). CISC stands for Complex Instruction Set Computing. CISC processors are good at handling long, complex commands in large numbers. The only drawback is that they do so at a leisurely pace.

In 1994 a new type of processor arrived. Developed jointly by Apple, IBM, and Motorola, and known as the PowerPC chip, it was based on a processor technology known as RISC (Reduced Instruction Set Computing). RISC processors can handle short, simple sets of commands very quickly. They are also cheaper to manufacture than CISC chips. Apple's Power Macintosh machines were the first to use a PowerPC processor. Meanwhile, Intel developed the Pentium Pro and Pentium II chips, both of which combine CISC and RISC technologies.

MULTIMEDIA COPROCESSORS

As multimedia continues to grow in importance, so processor technology is having to adapt to its specific requirements. In 1997, Intel launched the MMX chip – a Pentium chip with extra multimedia instructions built in. Intel's chip is part of a wider trend to boost the performance of multimedia by handing over its complex tasks to hardware rather than software. Many expansion cards now have special coprocessor chips that handle multimedia data, such as graphics or video, and speed up performance by taking the pressure off the main processor.

1985

CD-ROM
At the time of its arrival, a CD-ROM disc could hold about 20 times more data than the average hard disk.

1990

WINDOWS 3.0
Version 3.0 of Microsoft's operating system was the first truly effective version of the Windows GUI; PCs were now user-friendly. By introducing special support for multimedia hardware such as sound cards and CD-ROM drives, Windows 3.0 also laid the foundation for the development of multimedia software.

1994

RISC TECHNOLOGY
Manufacturers began moving toward using RISC processors in their machines. Apple used RISC technology in its PowerPC range and Intel also began to incorporate elements of RISC technology in some of its processors.

1997

MMX
Eager to improve the performance of multimedia on the PC, Intel developed a range of Pentium chips that use MMX technology. MMX chips contain extra instructions for handling video, graphics, and audio files efficiently. Appropriately written software can use these extra features to enhance the multimedia experience.

THE APPLE MACINTOSH

When Apple launched the Macintosh in 1984, they were confident that it would change the face of computing. The business community had bought wholesale into the IBM-compatible PC, with its text-based screens and complicated commands – but the Macintosh was a computer that had been designed to be user-friendly. With its easy to use GUI (Graphical User Interface), built-in sound, high-quality black-on-white graphics, and a new pointing device called a mouse, the Macintosh was a revolutionary machine, offering a number of features barely seen outside a research laboratory.

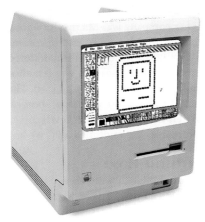

THE FIRST MACINTOSH
Often hailed as a design classic of the eighties, the Macintosh has evolved a long way from the 1984 model (right) to the way it looks today (below).

COMPUTING MADE EASY

Apple's aim was to take computers away from the experts and make them friendly enough for anyone to use – in the words of Apple's cofounder Steve Jobs, the Macintosh was a computer for "the rest of us." The GUI system, with its icons, menus, and mouse, made computing easy. New users could learn to work with the computer by following their intuition rather than a manual. Furthermore, the Macintosh looked different – its compact, all-in-one casing housed the computer, a small monitor, a speaker, and one of the first floppy disk drives to use today's plastic-cased disks. Many first-time computer users fell in love with the "Mac" immediately.

BUSINESS REJECTS THE MAC

If the Mac had caught on with business, it might have ruled the computing world. To commercial users, however, the Mac seemed too much like a toy to be capable of any-thing useful – the first Macs had no hard disk, were very short on memory, and were not cheap. More importantly, many firms had invested heavily in IBM-compatible PCs and the software to match, and Macs could neither run PC software nor read PC files.

Years later, PCs were to adopt many of the Mac's innovations, from GUIs and the mouse to built-in sound hardware and more. But for the time being, Apple and its ideas were locked out of the main market, and the Mac had to discover its following elsewhere.

POWER MACINTOSH
Apple's latest machines are based on the speedy PowerPC chip and offer impressive multimedia performance. Add-ons range from a TV tuner to a card that lets you use PC software.

AudioVision Monitor
The Mac AV monitor has a built-in microphone and stereo speakers.

CD-ROM Drive
As well as a CD-ROM drive, many Macs have special multimedia facilities such as video editing tools and high-quality sound.

PUBLISHING HITS THE DESKTOP

The Macintosh brought about a completely new use for computers – DTP (desktop publishing). DTP programs allow document pages to be laid out in the same way newspaper and magazine designers once used layout pads, scissors, and glue. The book you are reading was produced on a Mac with the aid of a DTP program.

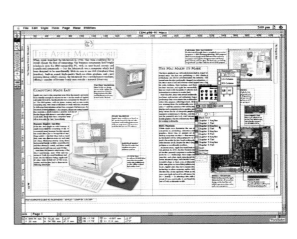

THE MAC MAKES ITS MARK

The Mac's graphical way with information had an impact in several areas. The first was publishing – DTP, or desktop publishing (see above), revolutionized the industry. The second area was education – the Mac's ease of use and obvious visual appeal was a big hit with children and their teachers, and Apple has successfully kept in touch with the needs of schools and universities to maintain its market lead.

From the start, Macs were natural multimedia machines, and teachers and enthusiasts began producing their own interactive multimedia with a Mac program called *HyperCard*. All that was missing from the multimedia mix was color – until the arrival in 1987 of the Mac II, which could display and manipulate photo-quality pictures. It was not long before the art of computer graphics switched from expensive workstations to the Mac, and designers rushed to use the powerful new tool. Largely because of its early ability to handle graphics, the Mac still remains the machine of choice for making multimedia.

HYPERCARD

Apple's *HyperCard*, the first multimedia "authoring" tool, imitates a card filing system – but to each card you can add sound and graphics, as well as "buttons" that spring you to other cards.

RISC VENTURES

While Apple now dominates the use of computers in publishing, education, and graphics, fewer than 15 percent of all desktop computers are Macs – they remain in the shadow of the vastly popular PC. As a result, the market for Mac-based multimedia titles remains small, despite the fact that the majority of titles are created using the Mac.

In recent years, Apple has tried hard to win ground and recover from diminishing sales. In 1994 it pioneered the use of RISC technology with the PowerPC chip at the core of its new Power Macintosh line, giving an immediate boost to the performance of multimedia on the Mac. Apple's next step was to license Mac technology to other companies, and in 1995 the first Mac clones appeared. In the same year, Apple released PC cards that enabled the Mac to run PC software, combining the best of both worlds. In 1997 Apple officially joined hands with its old rival Microsoft in a partnership designed to rejuvenate Apple's market presence and ensure that the same quality of software that is available for the PC will also be available for the Mac.

RISC
For more on RISC technology, see page 87

Motorola Processor
Apple steered clear of Intel, and stayed with Motorola's 68000 series chips – until Apple, IBM, and Motorola later created the PowerPC chip.

Color Graphics Card
Apple added color to the Mac in great style, with cards that can show over 16 million colors.

INSIDE A MACINTOSH
With the Macintosh II, Apple left behind the all-in-one box design of the first Mac and added expansion slots, color, and a lot more power.

Expansion Slots
The Mac II added room for upgrade cards that would improve the Mac's speed and graphics.

THE SEGA SATURN

Most games players think of the Japanese corporation Sega as the creators of Sonic the Hedgehog and longtime underdogs to Nintendo in the games console market. Sega actually began production in a different area of the interactive games sector – in video arcades, where its cutting-edge 3-D graphics technology has powered games far superior to any home video game. And now Sega's latest console, the Saturn, is powerful enough to bring their arcade games into the home.

Memory Cartridge Slot

THE SEGA STORY

Sega's first major assault on the console market came in the form of the Genesis (known in Europe as the Megadrive), the world's first 16-bit home console system. Launched in the United States in 1990, it was a massive hit with the games-playing public. The Genesis was cartridge-based, but in 1993 Sega introduced the Sega CD, an add-on CD-ROM player.

When 3DO technology was announced in 1992, Sega began planning its next console. Based on a 32-bit processor and a double-speed CD-ROM drive, the new machine's specifications would, Sega hoped, put it beyond the reach of the competition. Then Sony announced the PlayStation console, and reports of its revolutionary performance reached Sega's ears. In response to this unexpected and powerful new rival, Sega delayed the Saturn development program. It was too late to make major alterations to the system, but Sega decided to take the time to equip the new machine with an extra graphics processor; arcade-quality 3-D imagery was to be the hallmark of almost all of Sega's future games.

PROCESSING POWER

The Sega Saturn arrived in Japanese stores at the end of 1994, and proved to be as powerful as Sega had promised, thanks to a collection of seven specially designed main processors. The main processing power comes from two fast 32-bit RISC chips built by Hitachi. These perform the thousands of mathematical calculations that are needed every second to magnify and rotate two- and three-dimensional images at great speed. Specialized graphics tasks are handled by three separate graphics chips: a sprite chip, which moves flat animated characters around the screen, and two background chips, which share the task of drawing, rotating, and scrolling moving backgrounds. The two remaining processors are on the custom sound card – designed by audio experts at Yamaha – which offers sound performance superior to that of any other home multimedia player.

Joypad

Joystick

Six-player Adapter

OPTIONAL EXTRAS
The range of peripherals for the Saturn includes several alternative control devices for gaming enthusiasts and an adapter that enables up to six people (or 12 people when used in tandem) to connect their joypads for multiplayer games.

Mouse

Steering Wheel

WHAT IT CAN DO

The Saturn is first and foremost a games machine – but as with most other consoles, it plays audio CDs and, with an adapter, Photo CDs. However, it is unique in that it also acts as a karaoke player, by removing the voice track from ordinary music CDs. With an optional digital video card, the Saturn can play Video CDs and games that have video sequences built in, such as interactive movies. And with an extra modem, Saturn owners can access the Internet.

Sega capitalized on its arcade game pedigree by launching a range of arcade-style control devices – for example, a racing steering wheel – that enable the Saturn to imitate Sega's multiplayer arcade machines. In addition, Sega has adapted most of its most popular arcade games so that they work on the Saturn. As the success of a games console can depend simply on the popularity of the two or three big-name titles that are available for it, this is a significant advantage in a home console market that is much more crowded than Sega had at first anticipated.

SEGA RALLY
The racing game that took the arcades by storm can now be played at home on the Saturn. Fast-moving and detailed scenery and multiplayer action add to the racing excitement.

Performance Matters

 Processor
The Sega Saturn is powered by two main 32-bit RISC processors.

 CD-ROM
The Saturn has a double-speed CD-ROM drive.

 Sound
The Saturn's Yamaha sound card gives it 32 channels of CD-quality sound, MIDI music, and surround sound effects.

Graphics
The Saturn's three graphics processors produce fast and sophisticated 2-D and 3-D animation.

 Software
Most Saturn titles are action games. The Saturn can also play audio CDs, CD+Graphics, and with extra adapters, Photo and Video CDs.

 Linking
With extra adapters, up to 12 players can play together.

 Special Features
An optional memory cartridge allows users to save game data. With a modem, users can connect to the Internet.

FIGHTERS MEGAMIX
Sega's 3-D hand-to-hand combat game involves hundreds of realistic fighting moves and a constantly changing point of view that accentuates the 3-D graphics.

MANX TT
In this motorcycle racing game from Sega, players can try out the hazardous Manx TT track from the safety of their Saturn. The game offers a variety of tracks and bikes, and supports split-screen multiplayer racing.

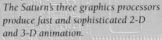

Multimedia-making is a young, dynamic, and fast-paced industry. This chapter shows how a multimedia encyclopedia and an interactive movie were made and then examines each multimedia element – authoring, text, sound, graphics, animation, and video – in turn to reveal the secrets behind some of today's best games and reference titles.

MAKING A CD-ROM

ROM FIRST IDEA TO FINAL product, most CD-ROM titles are between one and two years in the making. The multimedia production process combines the ideas and efforts of dozens of skilled individuals: designers, editors, animators, video and sound engineers, programmers, and producers. The industry is young, rapidly changing, and very competitive. As a result, multimedia companies are always looking for technological improvements and new title areas to explore that will give them the edge over their rivals. In this section, we show how two CD-ROM titles – an encyclopedia and an interactive movie – were made.

MAKING HISTORY

Dorling Kindersley's *Eyewitness History of the World* is one of the company's series of award-winning multimedia encyclopedias. The multiple challenge for its creators was to encompass a vast subject while keeping the information accurate, interesting, and interactive. Each of the encyclopedias in the *Eyewitness* series is based on an elaborate central console that offers different ways to explore a set of illustrated articles. What needed to be established initially for *History* was exactly how the information would be arranged and how the console would work. In multimedia production, thorough planning is vital, and so management put together a small team of editors and designers and gave it two months to generate and discuss ideas for the title.

PROJECT PROPOSAL

After trying out and rejecting many possibilities, the team reached its final proposal. The main console would enable the user to travel between ten themed periods in history – for example, the Age of Conquerors, (1100–1492), and Nations and Empires (1825–1900). A globe in the center of the console would make it possible to travel through the world history of each period. Arranged around the console would be a collection of artifacts (such as pieces of art, weapons, tools, and so on) that would change to reflect each period – the user would be able to choose any artifact to find out more about it. A small bookshelf would contain a Who's Who and guides to the history of Innovations, Everyday Life, and Culture, and a quiz machine would test the knowledge the user had acquired.

PLANNING MEETING
Once the overall structure of the title has been established, the team leaders meet to discuss the project in detail, to establish a production schedule, and to determine what the workload will be for each team.

Design
The design team is responsible for designing the title's interface and producing all the 2-D and 3-D graphics.

Resources
The resource teams produce sounds, animations, and videos for the title.

Production
The production team coordinates the different strands of the project and is responsible for keeping the title on schedule and within the budget.

Editorial
The editorial team structures the information content of the title.

Flowchart
The team leaders discuss a proposed flowchart of the title's interactive connections.

Interface
This designer works on the structure and design of the main console.

PROTOTYPES AND PREPARATION

Once management accepted the proposal, the next stage was to build a series of working prototypes. The editorial and design teams used the early prototypes to test and refine the way the title worked and looked, and the final version was used both to establish a design template for the rest of the project and to provide a means of demonstrating the product to the multimedia industry.

With the template for the CD-ROM established, preparation for the main production began. Each historical period had its own editor and designer. Working with a history expert, the editor began detailed research into the key events, inventions, and personalities of the period, at the same time gathering archive pictures and video footage. The designer worked on rough screen layouts for every article.

EARLY PROTOTYPE
Early prototypes are used to test the interactivity of the product. The multimedia elements are represented by sketches and placeholders.

Rolling Desk
In this prototype, a desk closes and opens to reveal a new time period.

PROTOTYPING
The design and editorial teams coordinate words, images, sounds, and moving pictures to build a prototype version of the CD-ROM.

Design Ideas
The design leader discusses the screen layout with an editor and a designer.

Authoring
The design and editorial teams use authoring software to build all the multimedia elements into one interactive program.

EVERYTHING ON PAPER FIRST
Before work on the multimedia elements begins, the editor-designer pairs prepare everything on paper – detailed plans that show exactly what text, still pictures, sounds, animations, and video clips are needed, and exactly where they belong.

Editor
The editor researches every topic and decides which multimedia elements to use.

Designer
The designer experiments on paper with design ideas for each screen.

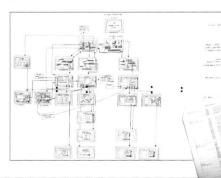

Navigation Blueprint
This is a template of how the user can navigate around the title.

Headword List
This is a list of every topic to be covered. Each will become an on-screen article.

Scamps
These are pencil layouts that show how the text and images will be positioned on every screen.

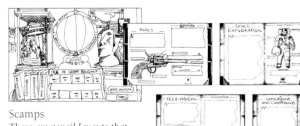

MULTIMEDIA RESOURCES

After planning each screen, the editorial team's next task was to research and commission the article text for it. Writing for a CD-ROM history of the world was not always straightforward – the writers had to present all the key information while keeping the articles short enough to allow space for screen images. The editors then edited each article and wrote quiz questions, index entries, and cross-references to other articles.

Meanwhile, the other teams set about creating their multimedia resources. The designers switched from paper to the computer screen to create the graphics; and the sound, video, and animation teams began work. By now, the combined development team had grown to 20 people, all of whom had new ideas and ways to improve the title they were working on.

SOUND
The sound team records a spoken narration of every article, as well as voice-overs for animations and video footage, and sound effects to accompany the user's progress through the title.

Sound File
Studio work takes up less than a third of the sound engineer's time. Most of the work is in editing and mixing digital sound files.

GRAPHICS
The designers build up the graphics for the console and all the articles by combining existing artwork and archive photographs with original 2-D and 3-D computer graphics.

VIDEO
The video engineer produces the clips to be used by editing together archive documentary footage. The computerized video clips need to be of high quality if the product is to succeed.

Digital Video
The video team uses computer video-editing software to digitize and edit the footage.

Animation Frames
The pencil animation frames are first digitized, then colored in using computer paint software.

ANIMATION
To produce the animations for the title, the animators combine the techniques of traditional hand-drawn cartoon animation with computer image manipulation and 3-D graphics.

BUILDING THE TITLE

While the resources were being prepared, the programming team worked on the company's "run-time engine" – the software that would play the finished title. The engine had been developed for earlier titles, to play them faster and more smoothly than authoring software can. The task now was to expand and adapt the engine to meet the specific interactive needs of the history encyclopedia.

As the required multimedia elements materialized, the editor-designer pairs began creating the final screens. To do this, they used specially modified page-layout software (which is normally used to put books and magazines together). This enabled them to lay out the images, cut the text to fit, and add hotspots and interactive links all at the same time. It also meant that the finished screens could be plugged directly into the run-time engine.

FINAL STAGES

The final months involved repeatedly testing and fine-tuning the title. As the programmers finished each new section of software code, the development team would test it to identify any bugs. The whole team also worked on refining the title's multimedia elements, functionality (the different ways a user can interact with it), and performance.

In the last month, a series of test releases of the title were burned onto gold master CD-ROMs and sent to a team of professional testers for checking. When the last gold master was declared bug-free, it was sent to the pressing plant for mass production.

Page File
This is an authored page. It can be plugged directly into the run-time engine (the software that will play the title).

LAYOUT AND AUTHORING
The designer and editor use modified page-layout software to compose the graphics and text for every screen, building in hotspots and interactive links at the same time.

TESTING
Computers as well as human beings are used to test the product. Here, a computer is clicking randomly on the screen and recording what happens.

BURNING THE MASTER
The final program is burned onto a gold master disc from which every marketed CD-ROM will be produced.

PROGRAMMING
The programmers work on adapting the existing run-time engine for *History*. This involves adding new kinds of functionality and fine-tuning the program for optimum performance.

Debugging
When the test program crashes or performs badly, the programmers often have to search through hundreds of lines of programming code to isolate the instructions that are causing the problem.

FILMING AT PINEWOOD

Pinewood Studios, home to the James Bond films, was chosen for the shooting of *The Darkening*, which took place over several months. The entire technical team normally required for a full-length movie was hired – assistant directors, cameramen, "sparkies" (electricians), and lighting engineers – and found themselves working for a computer games company. From their point of view it was business as usual, with one exception: in an interactive movie, each scene has to be filmed several times with different endings, to allow for the different choices the user might make when playing it. Because the player can choose to befriend or betray characters, the actors have to enact the same scene four or five times, with endings that vary from joyful triumph to painful death. According to John Hurt, one of the stars of *The Darkening*, such variations are, in fact, very rewarding because the actor is able to explore a role more thoroughly than is possible in a traditional movie.

POSTPRODUCTION

During filming, many scenes are shot against a blue background. Later on, in the post-production stage, a technique known as chromakeying is used to replace these blue backgrounds with computer-generated images, such as those created using 3-D modeling techniques. Also during post-production, many video sequences are made interactive: they are programmed to react when the player moves the cursor to a particular position. In some sequences, for example, the programmers will enable the player to talk to a character in the scene by moving the cursor over that character.

Chromakeying
For more on chromakeying, see page 153

DIGITAL VIDEOTAPE
The cameras used to shoot *The Darkening* were loaded with Digital Betacam videotape. This enables the video to be shot in a digital video format that computers understand.

BUILDING THE SET
A set designer from Pinewood Studios was called in to plan, then physically build, the sets for the filmed scenes.

Set Construction

Construction Team

Plan of the Set

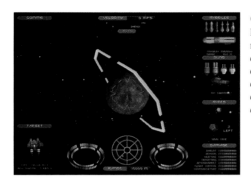

CUSTOM DATA
Players can choose how
much data is displayed
on their screen; for
example, they can
choose to view their
current missile count
or damage status.

Sound editing
For more on sound
editing, see page 126

SOUND AND MUSIC

Sound as well as video has to be added to the computer game. The
actors' voices are recorded at the time of filming; voice-overs and
sound effects are recorded later, onto DAT (Digital Audio Tape). One
problem is that most multimedia computers play sound through
accompanying small plastic speakers, so game developers go to great
lengths to optimize the sound quality possible with these speakers.
They use sound editing software to look for waveforms that expand
to the point where they distort – any waves that go over the
distortion limit are electronically corrected or smoothed out.

TESTING AND PUBLISHING

In the final stage of production, a multimedia game has to go through weeks of
testing. Playing *The Darkening* through just
once from start to finish can take nearly
50 hours. Even if there were no mistakes to
correct, it would still take one person several
weeks to check all the possible variations.
Instead, a team of youngsters is drafted for
the dream job of being paid to play games
all day. The testers note down any misspelled
words, any hitches in gameplay, any sounds
that crackle, and so on. The entire process is
then repeated for each different foreign
language version. Finally, when everyone is
satisfied, the master discs are created (the
game fills six CD-ROMs) and sent for
pressing, packaging, and distribution.

Sister Maria

Talk to Sister Maria

Exit to Customs

PLAYER CHOICE
During interactive scenes, players can
choose a course of action. In this scene,
moving the cursor over Sister Maria
causes her to turn toward you. Move the
cursor over the exit door, however, and
she turns away. The choice is yours.

Alternative Actions

TRADING
Successful trading is
an essential part of
The Darkening. Here a
player can buy or sell
a variety of spaceships.

Hiring the Cast

With a budget of around five million dollars,
Electronic Arts was able to hire leading actors.
In addition, 500 extras were chosen from
photographs sent in by agencies specializing
in striking and bizarre-looking characters.

Christopher
Walken

John Hurt

Clive Owen

THE ART OF SOUND

THE ENTERTAINMENT INDUSTRY has long appreciated that sound can enhance visual experiences. Even before the invention of a sound track on celluloid turned silent films into the talkies, the screening of movies was often accompanied by a piano or an orchestra. In today's multimedia titles, music and sound effects are used, as in the movies, to enhance the drama and realism of what the user sees – but now multimedia sound professionals are having to rise to a new challenge, one that is unique to the industry. Multimedia puts the user in control of the action, so it needs an interactive sound track.

LISTENING PLEASURE

Until recently, multimedia developers paid little attention to how their titles sounded. In their hurry to exploit the possibilities of 3-D graphics, animation, and video, they overlooked the potential of the audio track. Poor sound quality, music that stopped abruptly at the click of a mouse button, or silence, all betrayed a lack of attention to the user's listening pleasure. But as TV, film, and record companies have moved in on the multimedia act, sound production values have risen. Digital video discs, with their capacity for multichannel audio, will also increase the potential for quality soundtracks in multimedia titles.

ENHANCED ACTION
Interactive sound effects add realism to 3-D action games such as *Novastorm*, an early title from Psygnosis.

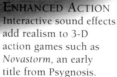

MIXING MUSIC
Jump, the David Bowie Interactive CD-ROM, by BMG, puts you in control of the mixing desk for one of his songs.

INTERACTIVE SOUND
In the best multimedia, music, dialogue, and sound effects are used not only to accompany the visual experience, but also to enhance interactivity. In 3-D games, the footsteps of an alien creeping up on you are created with stereo and Dolby-surround sound effects to reinforce the sensation of moving in three dimensions. Information titles use sound in a different way. For example, mouse clicks are often confirmed audibly and the transitions between screens may be accompanied by music. As well as adding to the experience, this fills the gap while the CD-ROM drive reads a new chunk of data. New techniques for streaming audio data over the Internet have even made it possible for World Wide Web pages to carry interactive sound.

Streaming
For more on streaming, see page 170

How Multimedia Sound is Made

Making sound for multimedia titles involves several distinct stages. This example follows the creation of a sound track to accompany an animated sequence.

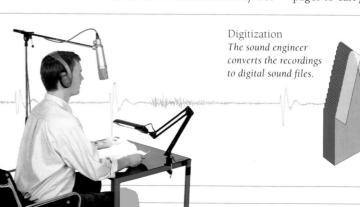

Digitization
The sound engineer converts the recordings to digital sound files.

Recording
In the studio, narration, dialogue, and sound effects are recorded with a microphone.

How Sound Works

Sound is produced when an object vibrates – for example, a spoon when it is dropped or a guitar string when it is strummed. These vibrations produce sound waves – waves of pressure which move through the air in all directions. When the sound waves reach your ear, they are converted into signals that are interpreted by your brain.

Recording for multimedia involves converting sound waves into two other types of signals – first into an analog electrical signal, and then into digital information that can be stored and manipulated by a computer. Eventually, when the sound is played back, the process will be reversed, and the digital sound converted back into sound waves.

From Sound Waves to Digital Sound

To record sound for multimedia, sound waves are converted first into an analog electrical signal, and then into digital sound. The three types of sound, and how they relate to one another, are shown here.

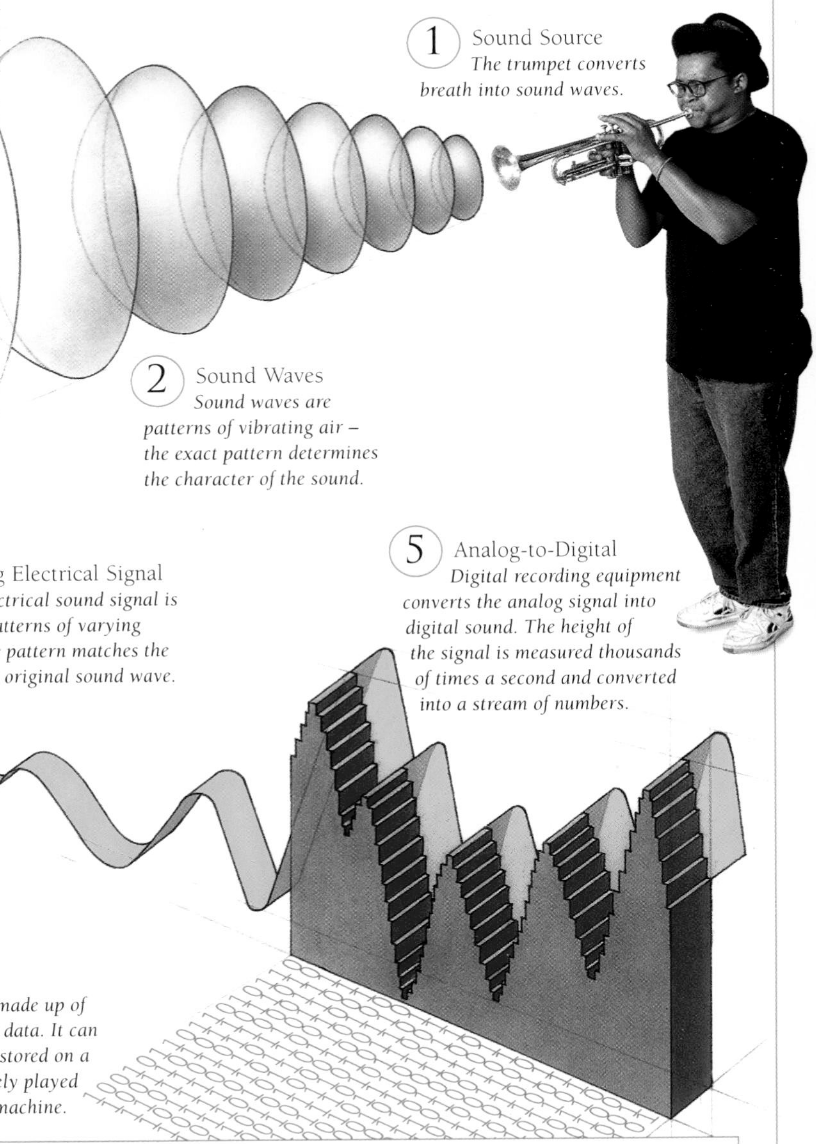

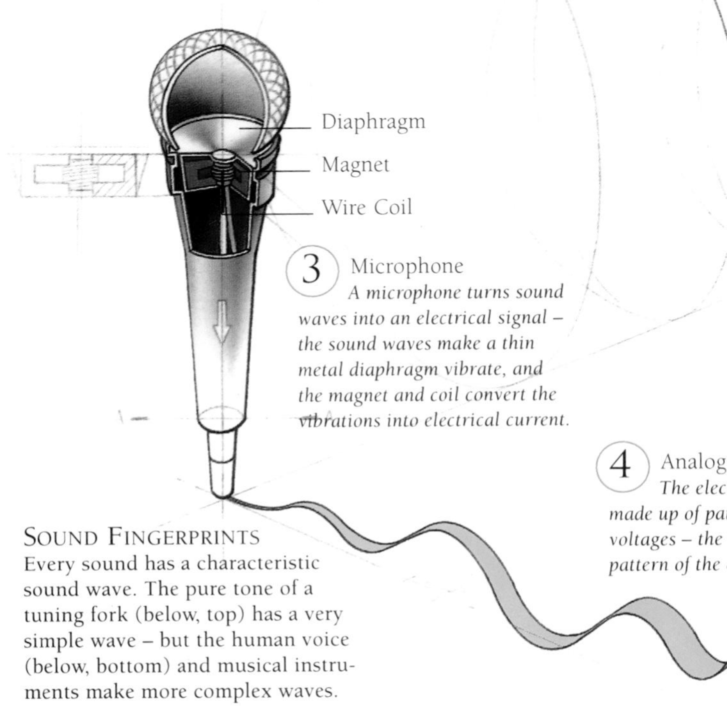

(1) Sound Source
The trumpet converts breath into sound waves.

Diaphragm
Magnet
Wire Coil

(3) Microphone
A microphone turns sound waves into an electrical signal – the sound waves make a thin metal diaphragm vibrate, and the magnet and coil convert the vibrations into electrical current.

(2) Sound Waves
Sound waves are patterns of vibrating air – the exact pattern determines the character of the sound.

(5) Analog-to-Digital
Digital recording equipment converts the analog signal into digital sound. The height of the signal is measured thousands of times a second and converted into a stream of numbers.

(4) Analog Electrical Signal
The electrical sound signal is made up of patterns of varying voltages – the pattern matches the pattern of the original sound wave.

Sound Fingerprints

Every sound has a characteristic sound wave. The pure tone of a tuning fork (below, top) has a very simple wave – but the human voice (below, bottom) and musical instruments make more complex waves.

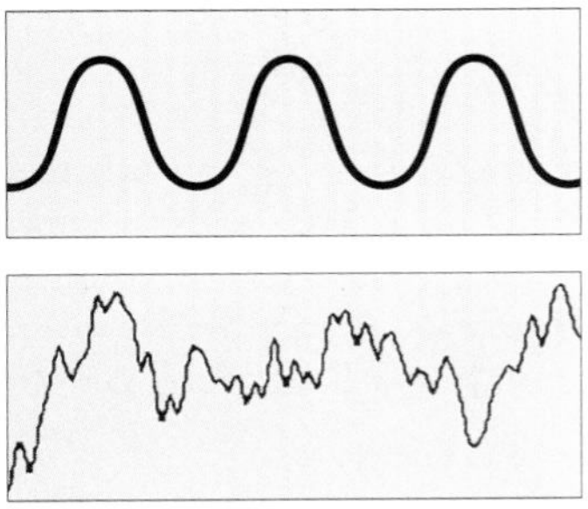

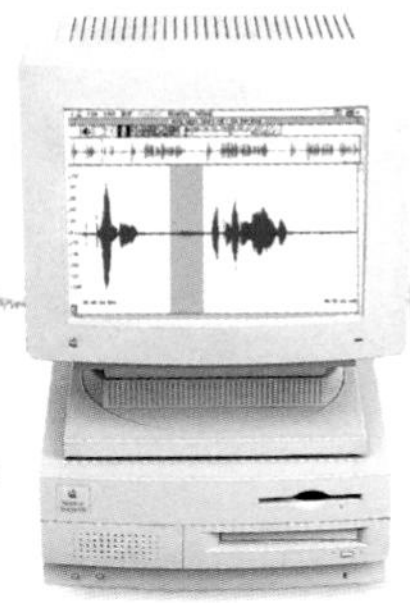

(6) Digital Sound
Digital sound is made up of the 1s and 0s of binary data. It can be read by a computer, stored on a CD-ROM, and ultimately played back by a multimedia machine.

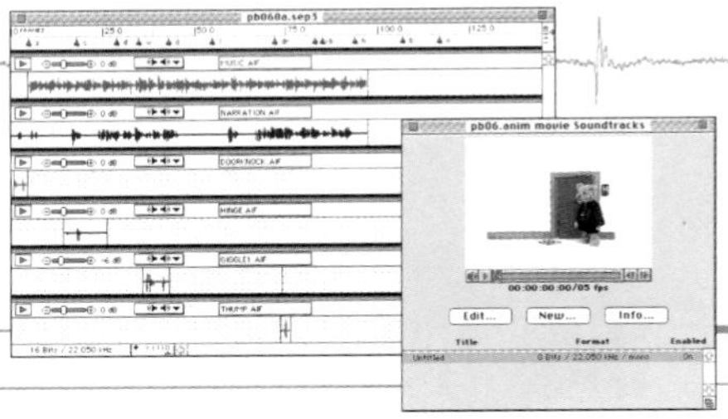

Mixing
The sound engineer adds the different sounds to the animation and mixes them into a final sound track.

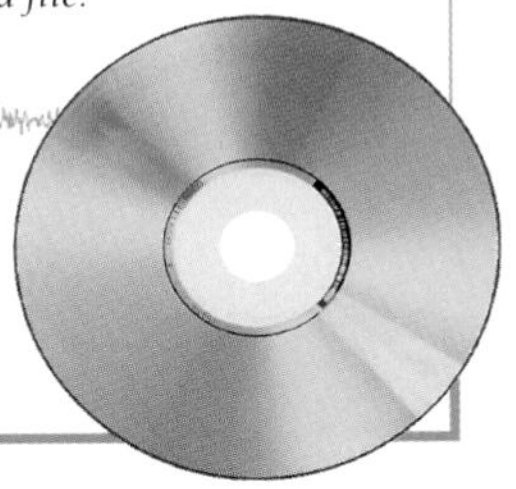

Onto the CD-ROM
The sound track is stored on the CD-ROM, not as a CD audio track but as a computer sound file.

Editing
Next, the sound engineer cleans up and edits the files on a computer.

THE RECORDING STUDIO

Step into a recording studio sound booth and the first thing you notice is the total silence – the background hum of everyday life is gone. The booth is not only completely soundproof, it is also "dead" – the walls and ceiling are built to absorb sound instead of reflecting it, so no echoes distort the recording. Even the furniture in the booth is kept to a minimum, because every surface affects the character of the recorded sound. This careful attention to the finer points of sound quality runs through the whole process of recording for multimedia.

THE VOICE ARTIST

Until recently, many multimedia titles used the vocal talents of the development team for their narration and dialogue, with predictably poor results. Sensibly, most multimedia makers today use professional voice recording artists, and even well-known actors such as Christopher Lee and Dennis Hopper are being enticed onto CD-ROM. Voice artists come in two varieties – narrators and character actors. Narrators are skilled at making documentary information punchy and clear, while character actors can breathe life into an animated character or dub a filmed performance.

PROFESSIONAL VOICES

A good narrator must have a "clean" voice, with little or no trace of an accent. A clean voice is free from sibilance (hissing s sounds), loud breaths between words, and mouth noise (the tiny sounds of tongue touching palate). For a character actor, however, irregularities such as these can lend an interesting individuality to the voice.

Good timing is critical, too. A narrator should be able to time the delivery of a paragraph to within half a second, while making subtle changes to the emphasis and tone of the script. Character actors need even better voice control to synchronize their performance to lip movements on video or animation.

RECORDING SOUND
The voice artist in the sound booth and the engineer at the recording desk work together to ensure a clean recording.

Monitor
This enables the actor to synchronize the voice-over with video or animation.

Microphone
This is positioned carefully: too far from the actor, background hiss is recorded; too close, it picks up the sound of the actor's mouth movements.

Headphones
These allow the actor to hear his or her voice as the microphone hears it.

Script
This may have to be rewritten on the spot to fit the available time, so a script editor is always on hand.

Sound Effects

Every multimedia studio has its sound effects library – thousands of clips on CD ranging from cartoon bangs, whizzes, and pops to earthquakes and police cars. But to get exactly the right effect the sound team often has to record the sound from scratch. However, it is not always as simple as staging events in front of a microphone. For example, when the sound team at Broderbund (makers of the adventure game *Myst*) recorded a crackling fire, the result just did not sound like the real thing. To get the sound they wanted, they ended up driving a station wagon over the gravel driveway outside the studio, and then slowing the recording down. For the sound engineer, this sort of ingenuity is called for every day. With a little bit of remixing, falling bags of sugar become footsteps, a flapping pair of leather gloves turns into an eagle taking off, and a box of vigorously shaken rocks is transformed into a marching army.

CRUNCHING SNOW
Engineers simulate the crunching noise of footsteps in soft snow by teasing a ball of cotton apart.

WRITING
For the sound of a quill pen writing on parchment, a plastic spoon is scratched against rough paper.

THE SOUND ENGINEER

Mixing Desk
At the mixing desk, the analog electrical signal from the microphone is equalized (sounds of different pitches are boosted or dampened).

Monitor
The engineer can see the sound levels of the recording on screen.

The bulk of the sound engineer's work happens after the recording session, when the sound files are edited and laid down as a sound track. At the recording stage, however, the engineer still has a vital task to perform: to capture the sound at the best possible quality. The engineer listens carefully for background hiss and distortion, and uses a range of tools to eliminate them. The analog electrical signal from the microphone is fed first into a mixing desk, then through a series of electronic filters that clean up the sound. Finally, the analog sound signal is converted to digital data.

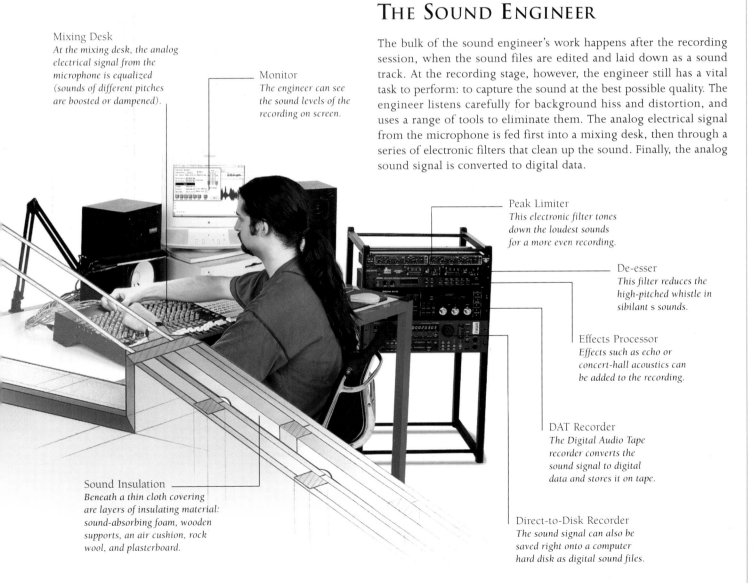

Peak Limiter
This electronic filter tones down the loudest sounds for a more even recording.

De-esser
This filter reduces the high-pitched whistle in sibilant s sounds.

Effects Processor
Effects such as echo or concert-hall acoustics can be added to the recording.

DAT Recorder
The Digital Audio Tape recorder converts the sound signal to digital data and stores it on tape.

Sound Insulation
Beneath a thin cloth covering are layers of insulating material: sound-absorbing foam, wooden supports, an air cushion, rock wool, and plasterboard.

Direct-to-Disk Recorder
The sound signal can also be saved right onto a computer hard disk as digital sound files.

SOUND CRAFT

After the recording session, the engineer listens to the sound files and decides which takes will go into the final sound track. Then the painstaking work of further cleaning up and enhancing the sound files begins. The engineer identifies individual problems and corrects each one using sound-editing software. The digital sound waves are shown directly on the screen, so flaws can be seen as well as heard – background hiss, mouth noise, and breaths between words all have distinctive shapes. The software's editing tools make manipulating the sound and correcting mistakes straightforward.

CLEANING UP SOUND WAVES

Every sound file is edited to remove mistakes and improve sound quality. Here the engineer is using Digidesign's *Sound Design* editing software to work on part of a recording – the words "cobweb" and "special laws" – that highlights many of the problems involved.

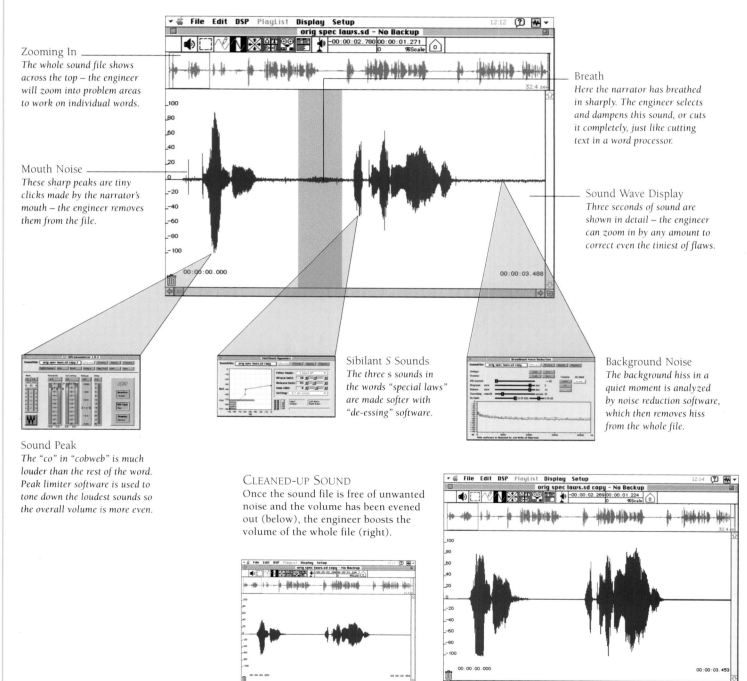

Zooming In
The whole sound file shows across the top – the engineer will zoom into problem areas to work on individual words.

Mouth Noise
These sharp peaks are tiny clicks made by the narrator's mouth – the engineer removes them from the file.

Breath
Here the narrator has breathed in sharply. The engineer selects and dampens this sound, or cuts it completely, just like cutting text in a word processor.

Sound Wave Display
Three seconds of sound are shown in detail – the engineer can zoom in by any amount to correct even the tiniest of flaws.

Sound Peak
The "co" in "cobweb" is much louder than the rest of the word. Peak limiter software is used to tone down the loudest sounds so the overall volume is more even.

Sibilant S Sounds
The three s sounds in the words "special laws" are made softer with "de-essing" software.

Background Noise
The background hiss in a quiet moment is analyzed by noise reduction software, which then removes hiss from the whole file.

CLEANED-UP SOUND

Once the sound file is free of unwanted noise and the volume has been evened out (below), the engineer boosts the volume of the whole file (right).

Timeline
This shows the animation frame numbers.

Music Track

Narration Track

Door Knock Sound Effect

Hinge Sound Effect

Laugh Sound Effect

pb060a.sep3

MUSIC
NARRATION
DOORKNOCK
HINGE
LAUGH

16 Bits / 22.050 kHz

LAYING TRACKS

The sound track is built up from the separate sound files – in this case, music, narration, and sound effects are being added to an animated sequence from the Dorling Kindersley title *P.B. Bear's Birthday Party.*

Animation Frames
Each sound effect is cued into a different frame in the animation.

CUING IN SOUND

Once all the voice-over and sound effects files have been edited, the engineer uses mixing software to put the final sound track together. At this point, specially recorded background music is also added to the mix. If the sound track is for video or animation, the first step is to watch the moving images frame by frame, deciding when to cue in each sound recording. The engineer then arranges all the sound files along a timeline, balancing the volume of each one. After checking that the finished sound track fits the moving images exactly, the engineer saves it as a single sound file.

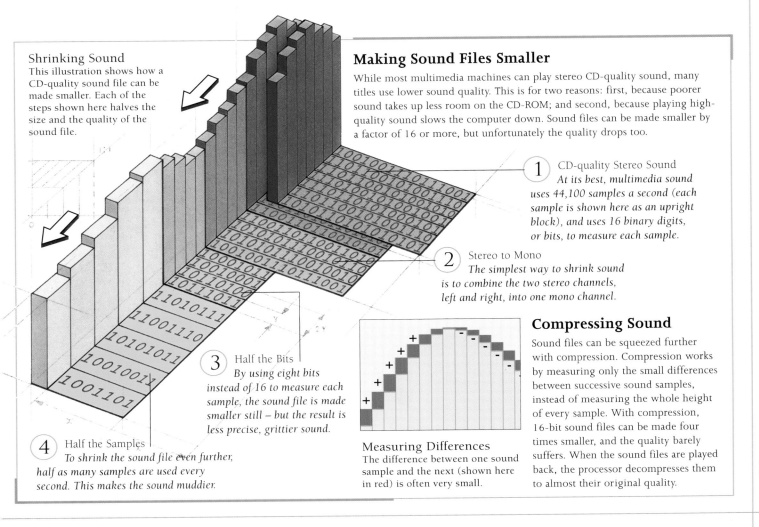

Shrinking Sound
This illustration shows how a CD-quality sound file can be made smaller. Each of the steps shown here halves the size and the quality of the sound file.

Making Sound Files Smaller

While most multimedia machines can play stereo CD-quality sound, many titles use lower sound quality. This is for two reasons: first, because poorer sound takes up less room on the CD-ROM; and second, because playing high-quality sound slows the computer down. Sound files can be made smaller by a factor of 16 or more, but unfortunately the quality drops too.

1 CD-quality Stereo Sound
At its best, multimedia sound uses 44,100 samples a second (each sample is shown here as an upright block), and uses 16 binary digits, or bits, to measure each sample.

2 Stereo to Mono
The simplest way to shrink sound is to combine the two stereo channels, left and right, into one mono channel.

3 Half the Bits
By using eight bits instead of 16 to measure each sample, the sound file is made smaller still – but the result is less precise, grittier sound.

4 Half the Samples
To shrink the sound file even further, half as many samples are used every second. This makes the sound muddier.

Measuring Differences
The difference between one sound sample and the next (shown here in red) is often very small.

Compressing Sound

Sound files can be squeezed further with compression. Compression works by measuring only the small differences between successive sound samples, instead of measuring the whole height of every sample. With compression, 16-bit sound files can be made four times smaller, and the quality barely suffers. When the sound files are played back, the processor decompresses them to almost their original quality.

THE DIGITAL ORCHESTRA

Although the compact disc was invented to carry high-quality recordings of music, ironically the music featured in multimedia is often of poor sound quality. This is because still and moving images take up so much space on most CD-ROMs that it is hard to find enough room to fit in music without sacrificing either quality or amount. The exception is music-based titles, in which only a small amount of multimedia interactivity is added to what is basically a musical album. Fortunately for multimedia software, there is a solution to the problem: a technology called MIDI, which allows hundreds of hours of music to be stored on one disc.

Music-based titles
For more on music-based titles, see page 58

MUSIC BY NUMBERS

MIDI (Musical Instrument Digital Interface) is an electronic language that gives musical instructions. In the same way that the notes on sheet music tell musicians what to do, MIDI data gives instructions to synthesizer keyboards, drum machines, and other electronic instruments. For multimedia, MIDI is convenient – not least because almost every multimedia machine contains a synthesizer on a chip. A whole symphony can be converted into MIDI and the chip can play it back, taking on all the parts of the orchestra. Unlike traditionally recorded sound, MIDI takes up very little room, because only one sound is stored for each instrument. MIDI does not slow down the rest of multimedia's activity; the synthesizer chip does all the work. It may not sound quite like the New York Philharmonic, but with today's synthesizer technology it can come surprisingly close.

How MIDI Works

MIDI is very similar to sheet music. The basic message simply says: play this note, this loud, for this length of time, on this instrument. It is one thing, however, to see a saxophone solo written as music notation, and quite another to hear a skilled saxophonist perform it. So MIDI also includes detailed information about how the music must be played, from the minute variations in pitch and volume of every chord to special effects that imitate the smooth slide between notes of a fretless bass guitar.

The more advanced MIDI synthesizer chips found inside games consoles and on the sound cards of multimedia computers can play up to 64 instruments at one time from an orchestra of between 100 and 500 prerecorded sound samples – everything from a harpsichord to a marimba.

MIDI music can be recorded without a real harpsichord or marimba in sight – all it takes is a talented musician and a setup like the one shown here.

Sound cards
For more on sound cards, see page 77

Sequencer
A computer running MIDI sequencing software is used to record and edit MIDI music.

MIDI Sound Device

MIDI Keyboard

THE MIDI STUDIO
The equipment shown here is the electronic equivalent of a composer's piano, a full orchestra, a recording studio, and a sound-editing suite.

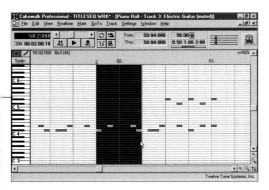

PIANO ROLL DISPLAY
As the composer plays each instrumental part, the notes are recorded on a grid that mimics a piano roll.

SCORE DISPLAY
Meanwhile, the sequencer keeps track of the score – classically trained musicians may prefer to edit the music by moving notes around staves.

MIXING DESK DISPLAY
Finally, the tracks are combined and the whole piece is mixed with an on-screen mixing desk.

RECORDING MIDI

Using sequencer software – the musical equivalent of a word processor – the multimedia composer records an electronic score, playing the part of one instrument at a time on the keyboard. The performance does not need to be perfect: the musician can edit any mistakes afterward, and the sequencer automatically corrects notes that are not exactly in time. Absolutely perfect timing may make the recording sound too clinical, so the sequencer can then add subtle computer-generated variations – oddly enough, this is called "humanizing." The composer can then edit the recording, by playing new notes into a section or by rewriting the score.

FLEXIBLE SCORE

MIDI music is most often used to accompany fast-paced action games and interactive adventures, where the music has to change to reflect the often unpredictable events on screen. To achieve this, many multimedia composers will record loops of music that can be repeated over and over – one for each scene, say. The composer may also record a set of tailpieces and musical links that can be played if the action is cut short or as a bridge from one scene to another. The end result is a flexible score – a toolkit of musical parts that is composed into a seamless flow every time the title is played.

The main drawback to MIDI is that the playback quality of MIDI files is determined by the quality of the synthesizer chip used inside the multimedia machine. Today's machines, with their sophisticated sound **Wavetable** hardware and wavetable technology, can at For more on wavetables, see page 77 last do justice to MIDI music, and the full sweep of the digital orchestra no longer has to sound like a bunch of electric organs.

MIDI Instruments

It is possible to record the sounds of an entire orchestra with a sequencer and a keyboard. However, a piano performance cannot reflect the intricate playing patterns of a saxophone or a guitar – to do this, musicians can use specialized instruments designed for recording MIDI. None of the tools shown here makes sound directly – instead they all make MIDI data.

Drum Pad
The drum pad simply records when and how hard it is hit and sends the information to the sequencer.

MIDI Guitar
This guitar has a special pickup that measures how hard and how fast each string vibrates.

Wind Controller
The saxophonelike wind controller measures the player's breath and records which keys are pressed.

GRAPHIC DESIGNS

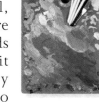

SUPERB GRAPHICS IS ONE OF THE keys to multimedia's appeal, and developers are well aware that the success of a title depends largely on the visual impact it makes. The multimedia industry attracts highly talented artists, who combine traditional skills as designers, illustrators, fine artists, and photographers with computer expertise. Each specialized area in the traditional arts is reflected in the computer graphics world by a different type of graphics software – powerful tools limited only by the artist's imagination. Here, a screen from Dorling Kindersley's *Eyewitness History of the World* shows how an artist can combine a range of techniques in creating a single image for the screen.

History of the World
For more on this title, see page 108

ART AND TECHNOLOGY

A decade ago, computer graphics were more a science than an art – graphics for computer games were mostly left to the programmers, while graphics for film and television were produced by a small number of designers using expensive, specialized computers. Since then, two things have happened. One is that graphics technology has made great progress. Designers now use desktop computers such as the Macintosh, which are powerful enough for all but the most intricate 3-D graphics work. The other development is that the software has become easier to use and is packed with tools and tricks that give designers infinite room for experiment and expression.

Macintosh
For more on the Macintosh, see page 90

BACK TO THE DRAWING BOARD

Accompanying this technological progress has been a return to more traditional design values – for, although computers make it easy to produce graphics, it takes a good designer to produce them well, instead of merely showing off what the software can do. As a consequence, the design team puts a lot of work into planning the overall look and feel of a title to make sure that the images are clear and consistent and do not swamp the rest of the information.

There are four main types of graphics software, three of which imitate equipment already familiar to traditional designers: the technical illustrator's drawing board, the photographer's darkroom, and the artist's easel. Many designers also prepare artwork by hand. The fourth type of software – and the only uniquely electronic art form – is 3-D graphics, which began as a tool for engineers and architects but is now at the heart of many of the most creative and exciting multimedia projects.

GRAPHIC TECHNIQUES
The historian's console shown here was created using a combination of all the main computer graphics techniques: drawing, painting, 3-D graphics, and image manipulation.

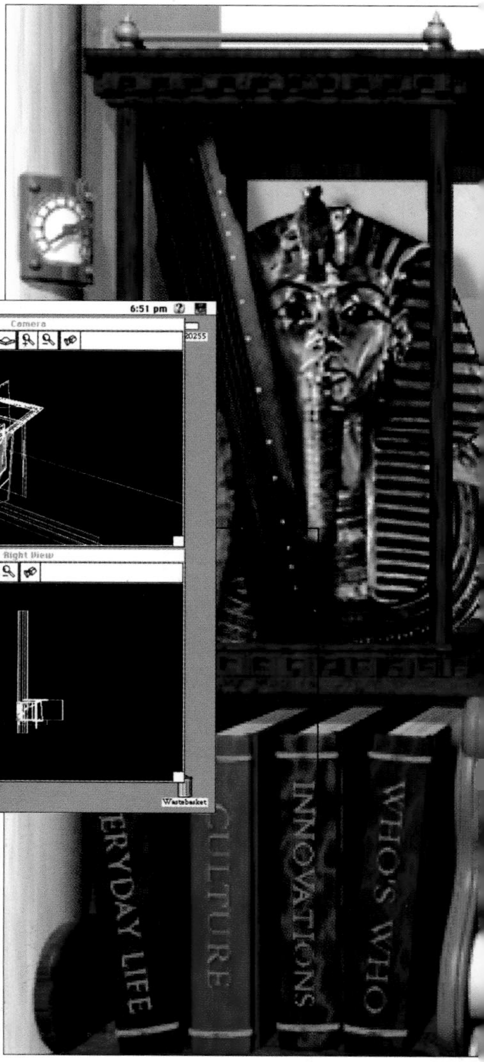

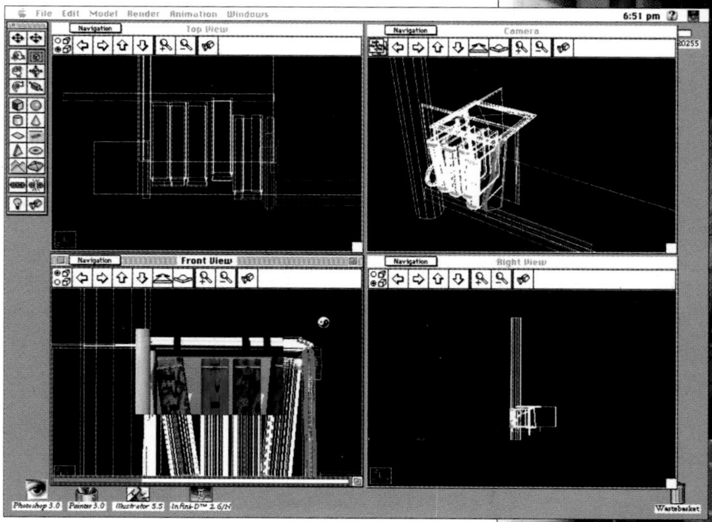

3-D Graphics
The body of the console, the globe, the display case, and the books shown here were all built as 3-D skeleton models. The artist added wood, leather, ivory, and brass surfaces to the models and wrapped the world map around the globe using the same 3-D graphics software.

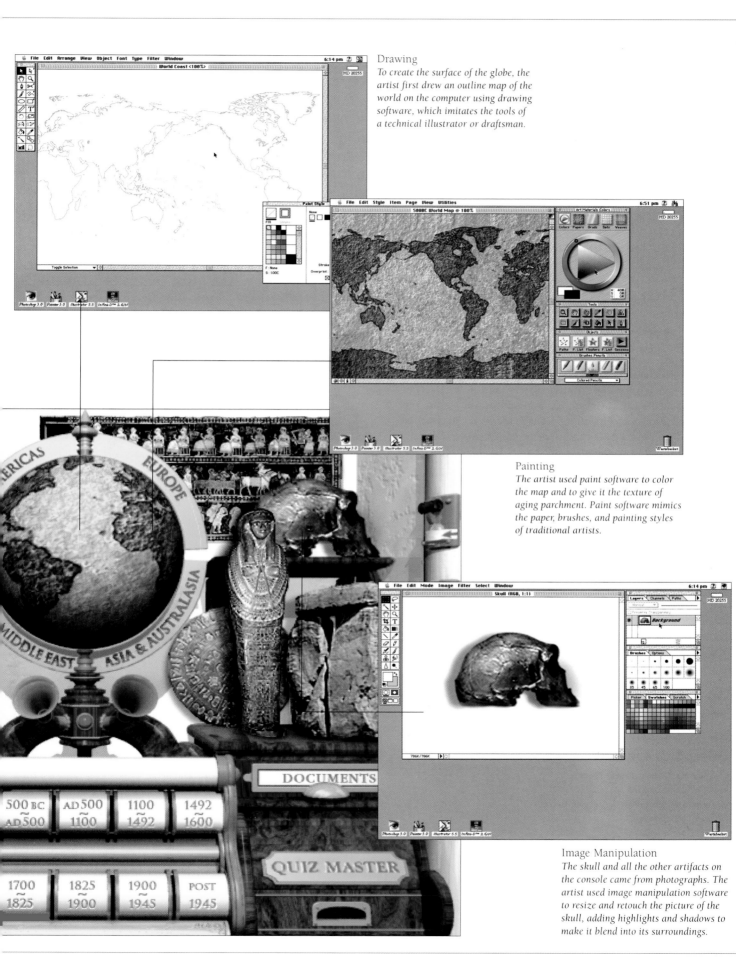

Drawing
To create the surface of the globe, the artist first drew an outline map of the world on the computer using drawing software, which imitates the tools of a technical illustrator or draftsman.

Painting
The artist used paint software to color the map and to give it the texture of aging parchment. Paint software mimics the paper, brushes, and painting styles of traditional artists.

Image Manipulation
The skull and all the other artifacts on the console came from photographs. The artist used image manipulation software to resize and retouch the picture of the skull, adding highlights and shadows to make it blend into its surroundings.

IMAGE MANIPULATION

Multimedia designers do not always create graphics from scratch on the computer – they often use photographs and hand-drawn artwork as the starting point for screen images. With a digital camera, a photographer can take electronic photos and feed them through a cable into a computer. More commonly, existing pictures are digitized with a scanner, which reads them in the same way as a color photocopier but creates digital copies instead of paper ones. Getting pictures into the computer is only the start of the process. With image manipulation ("imaging") software, the designer can use cameralike filters and all the tricks of a photographic darkroom to transform the original images into something totally new.

Desktop Scanner

THE ELECTRONIC DARKROOM

The first step in image manipulation is to improve the quality of the scanned image. A professional photographer may spend hours in the darkroom adjusting the brightness, contrast, and color balance of a single print, but with imaging software such as Adobe's *Photoshop* it can be done instantly with on-screen controls. With painting tools, the designer can also imitate the specialist techniques of hand finishing or retouching. For example, he or she can use an airbrush to paint over blemishes in the scanned image and add extra shading.

MAKING THE CAMERA LIE

Imaging software has a range of powerful tools called filters, which the designer can use to completely transform an image. Some of these imitate traditional camera effects, such as distortion with a fish-eye lens, while others do things that normal photography never could, such as making an out-of-focus picture sharper. By combining elements from different photos, and using filters and retouching tools, the designer can build a realistic scene that never actually took place. The coral reef from Dorling Kindersley's *Eyewitness Encyclopedia of Nature* on the opposite page shows how imaging software was used to create an underwater montage.

EFFECTS FILTERS
Designers can transform an image dramatically and instantly by using a range of software filters.

Encyclopedia of Nature
For more on this title, see page 22

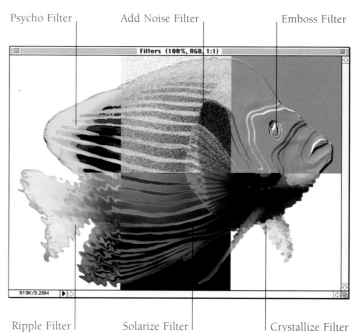

Psycho Filter   Add Noise Filter   Emboss Filter

Filters (100%, RGB, 1:1)

919K/3.28M

Ripple Filter   Solarize Filter   Crystallize Filter

Picture Quality

Most multimedia players cannot show photo-quality images, so the designer has to downgrade each screen picture in two ways. The first is to reduce its resolution – the number of pixels it contains. The second is to reduce its color depth – the number of different colors each pixel can have. The resulting image takes up a fraction of the storage space of the original.

Photo-quality Image   Lower Resolution   Fewer Colors

Cut-out Shark

PHOTOMONTAGE
This coral reef is a montage
of over 30 illustrations and
photos, assembled using
Adobe's *Photoshop* image
manipulation software.

Placing Images
*Each image is cut out from
its original photo and
placed into the montage.*

Background Layer
*The montage is made up of
many layers, one for each
image. The background layer
sits behind the others.*

Underwater Lighting
*Using an automatic lighting filter,
the designer adds highlights to
this picture of a fish. The fish is on
its own layer of the montage, so it
can be manipulated individually
without affecting the background.*

Lighting Filter

Color and Shading
*To make this fish blend into its
surroundings, the designer first
adjusts the colors in the image with
a filter, and then uses the airbrush
tool to add realistic shadows.*

Airbrushing Shadows

Original Artwork

Adjusting Colors

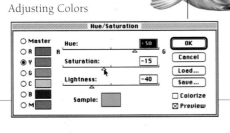

MODELING IN 3-D

Many of the most spectacular multimedia titles immerse the user in an artificial 3-D world that is as complex and richly detailed as it is beautiful, but creating an alternative reality is not as difficult as it seems. Even so, sometimes it takes a while for designers who are used to flat images to become accustomed to working in three dimensions – in fact, multimedia developers often employ trained architects to create 3-D designs, because architects are better able to visualize spatially. Imagination is allowed free rein, because the artificial world is not constrained by the laws of the real world; the software used to make 3-D models is powerful enough to turn almost anything the designer can think of into an almost tangible artificial reality.

WIREFRAME MODELS

Modeling software creates an imaginary three-dimensional space for the designer to work in. Every object in the space is represented as a set of points, which are joined to make an outline framework of straight lines. This is known as a wireframe (see opposite page). The whole 3-D world and all the characters in it are built up as a series of wireframes, to which the designer can add artificial surfaces, textures, and lighting to make a realistic final scene.

MAKING A WIREFRAME

The first step is to build a wireframe model. The example shown here is a console from a prototype of Dorling Kindersley's interactive 3-D "museum" *Eyewitness Virtual Reality Cat*. To construct the console, the designer used Specular International's *Infini-D* modeling software. Building a simple model is easy because the designer can choose from a set of basic shapes – spheres, cylinders, cubes, and so on – which can be placed on the screen, moved, and joined, or stretched and reshaped to create new shapes. By combining several basic shapes with a few more complex techniques, the designer can build up the wireframe of the console.

3-D CONSOLE
This information console from a prototype of Dorling Kindersley's *Eyewitness Virtual Reality Cat* was built as a 3-D model, using modeling software.

Virtual Reality Cat
For more on this title, see page 28

3-D COORDINATES
A 3-D model consists of many points in imaginary space. This cube is defined by where its corners are – the position of every corner is measured in each of the three dimensions X, Y, and Z.

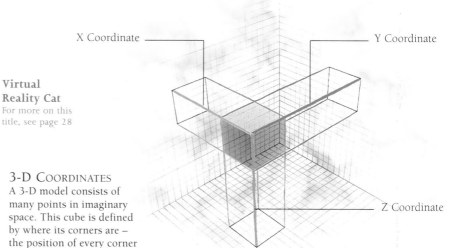

X Coordinate — Y Coordinate — Z Coordinate

Modeling Made Easy

Building 3-D models from scratch is time-consuming, but there are short cuts. Some 3-D graphics companies sell ready-made wireframes, which the designer can adapt. The alternative is to use a 3-D digitizer to take a wireframe from a real object – the designer touches the object repeatedly with the stylus on the end of the digitizer arm, and the computer measures the position of the stylus in space. With enough points, the designer can build a whole model.

Catalog of Ready-made Wireframes

3-D Digitizer

BASIC SHAPES

The designer uses 3-D modeling software to create the wireframe for the console (left). Working with a tool kit of basic shapes, the designer can move and reshape each object in the 3-D space of the program. Each of the building blocks below corresponds to the same-colored shape(s) in the model.

Sphere Tool
The sphere tool creates a globe of any size. Inside the computer's 3-D world, a perfect sphere is stored, but on the screen it is drawn with straight lines as a wireframe outline.

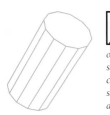

Cylinder Tool
The designer uses this tool to create the fluting on the side of the console and the struts that support the top. Once a cylinder has been placed, it can be stretched to the right dimensions and then moved into position.

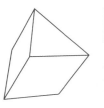

Extrude Tool
This tool adds simple depth to any flat shape. To make the top of the console, the designer draws a triangle and then stretches it into three dimensions with the extrude tool.

Lathe Tool
This tool makes a flat shape three-dimensional by rotating it in space. Here, the designer uses a circle as the starting point to make a doughnut ring.

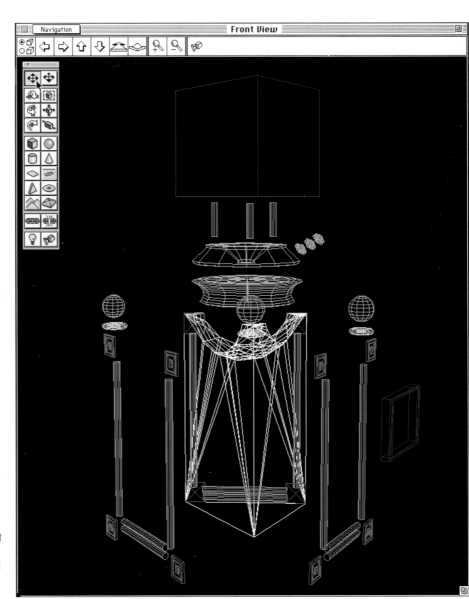

COMPLEX SHAPES

As well as combining simple building blocks, the designer can use some advanced modeling techniques to create the more complex shapes in the console.

Lathe Tool
To make the console's pivoting center, the designer uses the lathe tool again, this time changing the starting point to the shape shown at right.

Freeform Tool
The designer can create a new shape from scratch by drawing cross-sectional blueprints on the screen. Here, the designer is working on a sideways view (right).

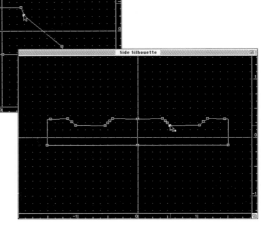

LIGHTS, CAMERA...

Once the model of the console is ready, the designer turns the computer's 3-D space into a photographer's studio by adding lights and a camera. These are small wireframe models that behave like the real thing. The position of the camera will determine the viewing point for the final image, and the light sources will illuminate the scene – they can imitate anything from the warm glow of a bedside lamp to the focused beam of a searchlight.

Light Angle

Light Focus

Light Color

RENDERING

The wireframe model still only shows an outline. To see the solid console under the lights, the designer takes a picture with the camera. This is called rendering. Seeing the rendered image enables the designer to try out different surface textures – such as ivory, wood, or concrete – on the model, and to adjust the wireframe and lighting.

There are three ways to render the object (see below). Flat shading is the fastest but crudest method – it treats every surface on the wireframe as a flat shape and fills it with a block of color. Curved shading goes a step further by blending the colors at the edges of each shape to make the surfaces appear smoother. Once the designer is happy with the model, surfaces, and lighting, the whole scene is rendered using the best (and slowest) method of all – ray tracing.

Raytracing retraces the exact path of every single ray of light that hits the camera, following each one in turn as it bounces off the surfaces of the object. As a result, the final image is highly detailed and very realistic, but on average it involves tracing the paths of over 300,000 rays. This can take a desktop computer days – so designers either use a powerful workstation computer or link several desktop computers together.

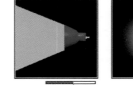

SPOT LIGHTING
The designer places one or more light sources in the 3-D space. By adjusting the angle, focus, and color of each light, it is possible to re-create almost any real-world lighting effect.

Light Source

CAMERA ANGLES
The designer places a camera into the 3-D space (above) and then looks through it at the wireframe console (right) to check the camera's position.

Camera

Camera View

Flat Shading

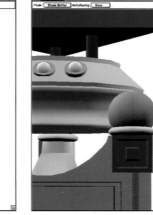
Curved Shading

Ray tracing

THREE WAYS TO RENDER
The three main rendering methods are flat shading, curved shading, and ray tracing. The first two methods are quick ways to test the wireframe, camera position, and lighting. They also give the designer an opportunity to experiment with colors and surface textures. Ray tracing is used to create the final image – it is by far the slowest technique, but it accurately draws in all the shadows, reflections, and highlights in the scene

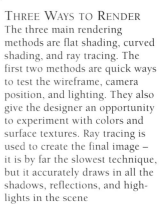

Adding Surfaces

The designer can attach realistic surfaces to any part of a model. Each different surface has its own coloring, texture, transparency, and reflectivity, and each of these properties can be adjusted. To try out new surfaces on the model, the designer has to render it again.

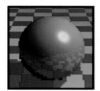

Brass

Eggshell

Blue Plastic

Glass

Strawberry

Spruce

Water Ripple

Coral

Emerald

Ball Bearing

Concrete

Mirror

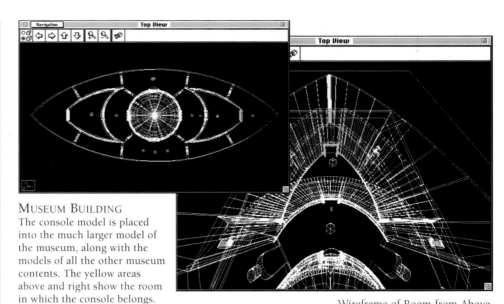

MUSEUM BUILDING
The console model is placed into the much larger model of the museum, along with the models of all the other museum contents. The yellow areas above and right show the room in which the console belongs.

Wireframe of Room from Above

THE FINAL RENDER
The completed scene is ray traced. Because this is so time-consuming, designers often link several desktop computers together; each one renders a fraction of the image at a time.

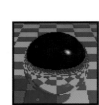

Cat Fur
This is a photograph of a real piece of fur. The designer has digitized the photograph, made it into a new surface type, and applied it to the top of the console.

Rendering in Squares
Each of these squares is being rendered by a different computer. When a computer has finished one square, it moves on to another.

Lynx
This picture is a 3-D model of a frame, in which hangs a flat digitized photograph of a lynx.

CREATING PANORAMIC MOVIES

The graphics and highly rendered 3-D models of the multimedia designer can be used to create virtual panoramic environments, known as QuickTime VR (virtual reality) movies. These give the viewer the impression of being immersed in a 360-degree environment, able to interact with objects, zoom in and out, and maintain complete control over their direction of movement. Users can stand in the middle of a room, say, then turn to see what is behind them; click on a door and go outside; hear sounds from different directions and see people or objects moving. Its creation demands experience in image manipulation, 3-D modeling, and special VR authoring software.

THE WHOLE PICTURE
This illustration shows how a 360-degree panorama of a lounge scene can be constructed from a series of overlapping images. The example shown is from Dorling Kindersley's *Eyewitness Children's Encyclopedia*.

CAPTURING THE MATERIAL

The first step in creating a VR movie is to build up a 360-degree picture of the chosen environment, by placing a camera at a fixed point and rotating it on a level plane, taking enough shots to show the full circular panorama. The number of shots needed to achieve this depends on the angle of the camera lens: a wide-angle lens requires fewer turns than a standard lens. Once the individual images have been acquired, they must all be "stitched" together to form a single, continuous image.

VR movies can be created by photographing real-world environments, or by using 2-D artworks or 3-D models that have been created with 3-D modeling software. A major advantage of using artificial rather than real-world scenes is the greater degree of control it affords. The position of objects can be fixed, because an artwork is not subject to unpredictable intrusions by people or animals, and changes in the weather do not affect the lighting conditions or the exposure time.

Rendered Views
Each shot is rendered by the 3-D modeling software once the view of the wireframe model has been captured.

USING 3-D MODELS

The principles involved in capturing material using 3-D modeling software are no different from using a real-world environment. The designer takes still shots of the environment by placing the software's computerized camera in a central position inside the model, and then electronically photographing the view from each angle as the camera is turned through 360 degrees.

3D Modeling
For more on 3-D modeling, see page 136

Angle of View
Each image represents one turn of the camera. The lounge panorama is made up of 24 different shots.

SETTING UP THE CAMERA

The images on the right show two corresponding views of the lounge in Dorling Kindersley's *Eyewitness Children's Encyclopedia*. The designer uses these views to set up the 3-D modeling software's camera.

Computer Camera
The designer sets the position of the software's camera using a plan view of the model. The position ensures a good view all round and is not too close to any one object.

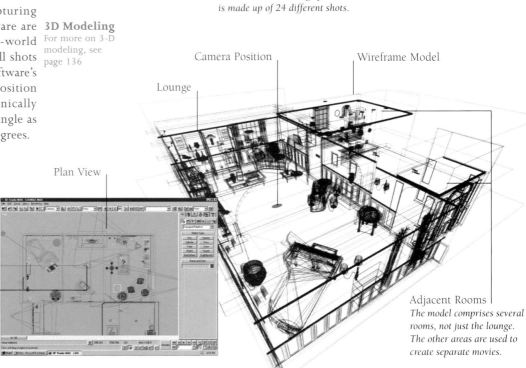

Camera Position

Lounge

Wireframe Model

Plan View

Adjacent Rooms
The model comprises several rooms, not just the lounge. The other areas are used to create separate movies.

Picture Overlap
The degree of overlap between each image can vary but should remain constant from shot to shot.

THE STITCHING PROCESS
Once the designer has acquired the individual shots for a panorama, special stitching software is then used to join the separate images together. This software blends together the edges of consecutive images, using the overlapping areas between each frame to work out exactly where the edges meet and to find the best fit. In the process, the software may slightly warp or distort the images so that the eye does not perceive the join. It also removes blemishes and graduates the image colors where necessary. The result is a long, linear image. This image is then converted into a 360-degree panorama using the stitching software to blend the two outer edges – which may not match exactly – and reconstitute it into a single, cylindrical image format that can be viewed using special VR movie software.

Warp Factor
Once all the images have been stitched together, warping and distortion are usually visible. This is a product of the cylindrical exposure, in the same way that a two-dimensional map of the world distorts the shapes of continents when compared with a globe.

PANORAMIC CAMERAS
By far the simplest way to capture material for VR movies is to use a special panoramic camera. Mounted on a sturdy tripod, such a camera need take only one single photograph along a length of film as it swings its lens through 360 degrees. In a single, continuous turn the camera avoids the need for the complex calculations, overlap, and stitching that other methods require.

Tripod

Camera Lens
A narrow slit restricts the angle of view as the camera rotates.

Motor
An internal motor rotates the camera on its head.

Panoramic Film
This panoramic film of the the Costa Rican rainforest can be easily wrapped around to form a cylinder.

ADDING ATMOSPHERE
The completed VR movie gives the user the feeling of being at the center of the environment. To enhance the immersive experience, designers may embed multimedia components such as sound and video into their panoramas. As the user moves around, sounds may change, or become louder or softer, to emphasize the feeling of movement.

Interactive Elements
Multimedia elements can be attached to special "node" points by placing a hotspot over the designated area and assigning an event to it. Here, clicking on the piano brings up a box offering more information.

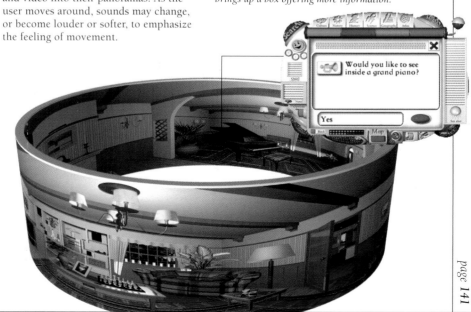

Would you like to see inside a grand piano?

Yes

INSIDE ANIMATION

MULTIMEDIA COMBINES TWO very different animation techniques, one old and one new. First, there is the hand-drawn animation of cartoons – Disney-style animated characters are used in multimedia software as everything from friendly on-screen teachers to the heroes of interactive cartoon adventures.

The other, far newer, technique is computerized 3-D animation, which is used to create most of today's fast-moving action games. Between these apparent extremes of art and technology, however, multimedia animation encompasses a wide range of other techniques, all of which demand creativity, ingenuity, and skill.

CARTOON ANIMATION

The most straightforward type of multimedia animation is the cartoon, which is produced in a very similar way to a cartoon for the movies. First, a team of animators draws every frame of the action by hand – this can mean as many as 25 frames for every second of animation. The next step is to trace and color in each frame. While many traditional animation companies still use armies of artists to do this, multimedia animators digitize their drawings with a scanner and use paint software to color them.

INTERACTIVE CARTOONS

Many multimedia titles, especially animated adventure games, have cartoon characters that the user can control. These titles use a technique called sprite animation. A sprite is an animated cut-out character (or object) that is moved over a stationary background. Each sprite consists of a tool kit of all-purpose animation sequences – running, jumping, fighting, for example – that are played in response to the user's actions.

TRADITIONAL ANIMATION
This noninteractive scene from the LucasArts cartoon adventure game *Full Throttle* was prepared using many of the traditional techniques of movie animators.

Background
While the sprite moves, the cartoon backdrop stays fixed.

Sprite
Only the sprite is animated.

SPRITE ANIMATION
Many interactive games use sprites – user-controlled animated characters. Here, the hero of the LucasArts cartoon adventure *Day of the Tentacle* is shown in several different positions.

MOVING IN THREE DIMENSIONS

Creating high-quality 3-D graphics requires a lot of computing power – and making them move requires even more. When the animator has built all the 3-D models for an animation and programmed in the movement, it can take a computer hours, or even days, to render (draw) every frame. Despite these enormous time demands, this sort of "prerendered" 3-D animation is often used to create the spectacular opening sequences of action games. It cannot, however, be used for the action itself. This requires another style of animation that a multimedia machine can draw very quickly in response to the player's actions – real-time 3-D.

3-D graphics
For more on 3-D graphics, see page 136

REAL-TIME 3-D

To make real-time 3-D animation possible, animators have had to develop many new techniques. Most 3-D action games are built around specially written software called a graphics engine that speeds up the animation. Many multimedia players, most notably consoles, include extra hardware designed to accelerate 3-D animation even more.

But producing real-time 3-D graphics also means taking shortcuts with the animation; these include using far simpler 3-D models and cruder rendering techniques. Although this makes the graphics appear more blocky, the movement is much more realistic.

3-D action games
For more on 3-D action games, see page 46

Consoles
For more on consoles, see page 92

PRERENDERED 3-D ANIMATION

This footage from Mirage's *Rise of the Robots (The Director's Cut)* shows the high level of detail that can be used in noninteractive animated sequences, where the 3-D animation frames have been prepared in advance.

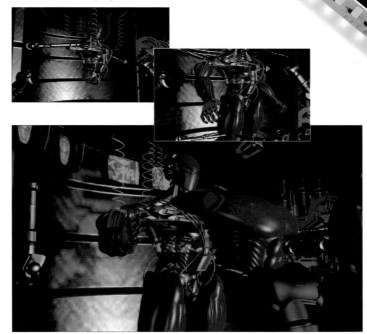

DRAWING 3-D QUICKLY

The space combat simulator *X-Wing* from LucasArts draws the 3-D view from the pilot's cockpit several times a second. The spacecraft shown flying past is built from fairly simple 3-D shapes so that the game can draw the pilot's view quickly.

MIXING 2-D WITH 3-D

Dark Forces, by LucasArts, uses a combination of 3-D graphics and flat cartoon sprites – the player moves through a 3-D environment that is drawn in real time, but the characters in the game are all flat cutouts.

3-D World
As the player moves around the 3-D world, the game constantly redraws the player's view.

2-D Sprite
Here, the sprite of the enemy soldier is simply enlarged as it gets closer to the player.

CARTOON ANIMATION

Many of the traditional functions of cartoon animators can now be performed using computers – teams of animators slaving away, tracing and coloring frames by hand, can be replaced with just a few skilled computer artists; this makes the process of creating an animation much quicker and easier. Even so, animators still prefer to use the old methods and materials – for example, they would rather draw on paper than on a screen. Titles such as Houghton Mifflin's *American Heritage Children's Dictionary* shown here demonstrate the blend of long-practiced human artistry and computerized assistance that is unique to multimedia animation.

OLD AND NEW TECHNIQUES

The first step in producing an animation of any kind is planning: the animator produces a storyboard of the sequence and a set of rough sketches of the characters. Then he or she begins drawing the actual animation frames as pencil outlines. To ensure that the movement is accurate, the animator first draws the "key frames" – every fourth frame, say – to fix the overall movement, and then draws all the frames in between.

A traditional animator would then hand over the pencil frames to an army of junior animators, who would first trace every frame in ink onto a sheet of clear plastic called a cel, and then color in every cel in paint. In multimedia animation, these stages can be carried out in a fraction of the time with the help of computer paint software.

CREATING A CHARACTER
The animated dolphin in Houghton Mifflin's *American Heritage Children's Dictionary* was created using cartoon animation techniques.

SCANNING IN
Once the pencil frames are ready, the animator digitizes them with a scanner and feeds them into the computer.

Animation Paper
The animator uses special translucent paper that is sometimes called onion skin.

Animator's Light Box
The light box enables the animator to see through a stack of several frames. Seeing through key frames makes it easier to draw the in-between frames.

Pins

MAKING FRAMES
The animator draws every frame of the dolphin animation by hand at a light box. A set of pins keeps the frames lined up with each other, and the light box illuminates them from behind.

Rough Scan
When the frames are first scanned in, they are of poor quality and need cleaning up.

Line Work
The first stage is to redraw the lines with a solid, even stroke.

Pencil Tool

Airbrush Tool

Coloring Up
Next, the animator fills the frame with instant color, using a fill tool, then adds shading with an airbrush tool.

PAINTING THE FRAMES

The animator does all the line work and coloring in using the paint tools in Adobe's *Photoshop* image-manipulation software. When all the frames are finished, the animator cuts the dolphin out of each one and places it into a rectangular cutout of the background.

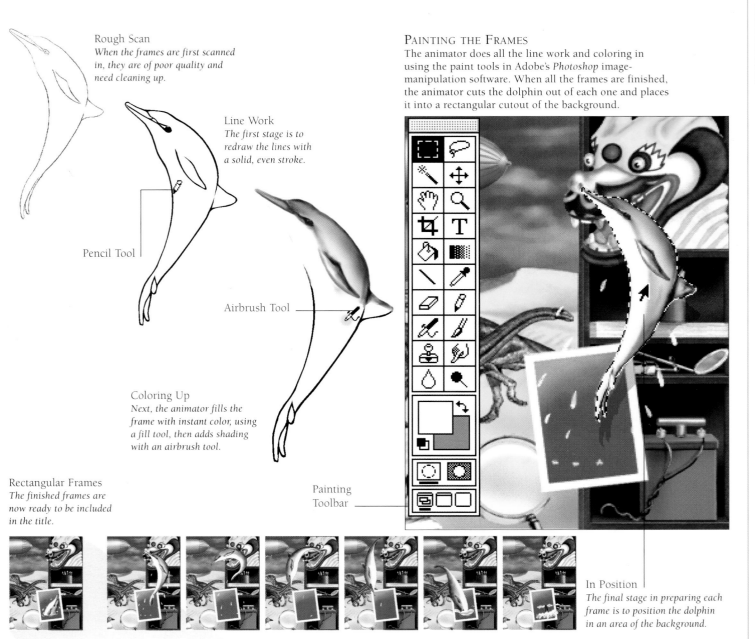

Painting Toolbar

In Position
The final stage in preparing each frame is to position the dolphin in an area of the background.

Rectangular Frames
The finished frames are now ready to be included in the title.

AUTHORING

Finally, the animator uses Macromedia's *Director* authoring software to place the set of rectangular frames as a single animation into the title and create a hotspot that will launch the animation.

Animation Frame
The first frame of the dolphin animation is put into place on the screen.

Hotspot
The animator draws a hotspot around the card. When the user clicks here, the animation will be activated.

ANIMATING 3-D MODELS

For cartoon animators, making drawings move well is a straightforward matter, the essence of their art – but animating in three dimensions presents major problems. To create a moving character, the animator starts by building it as a 3-D model. The next step is to animate it, but getting a 3-D jointed skeleton on a computer screen to follow natural movement patterns is not easy. The second problem is making 3-D models in such a way that the game software can draw them from scratch several times a second. Fortunately, both problems have their solutions, as Argonaut/GTE's martial arts combat game *FX Fighter* shows here.

3-D model
For more on
3-D models,
see page 136

CAPTURING MOTION

Some 3-D animators are very successful at re-creating the subtleties of human motion purely from their own observations. Others use a shortcut – a technique called motion capture. Instead of watching human movement, these animators film an actor going through a set of choreographed moves while wearing a special motion capture suit: each of the actor's joints – shoulder, wrist, knee, and so on – is represented on the suit by a large white dot, and when the actor moves, the positions of the dots show the key stages in the movement. The animators then use a computer to analyze the movements and fit them to the 3-D models.

Actor
The actor is filmed going through one of the hundreds of martial arts moves that will be used in the game.

Motion Capture Suit
This highlights each of the actor's joints.

FIGHTING MOVES
Each of the characters in Argonaut/ GTE's *FX Fighter* has a unique set of fighting moves. To make these realistic, the animators film real martial arts experts in action, then use a computer to re-create the same motion with a jointed 3-D skeleton.

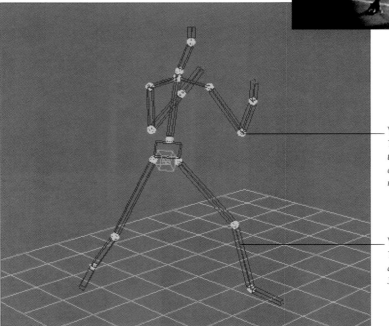

White Dots
The computer first re-creates the position and movement of the white dots on the motion capture suit.

Wireframe Skeleton
The computer then joins the dots together to form a crude 3-D wireframe skeleton.

Matchstalk Moves
The skeleton's movements accurately reflect the original fighting sequence.

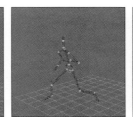
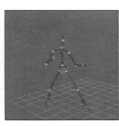

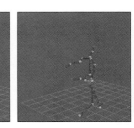

SIMPLE MODELS

The next step is to fit the moving skeletons to 3-D character models. For every character, two models are built. The first is highly detailed and is used for the game's noninteractive title sequence; each frame of animation undergoes high quality rendering (which adds highlights and shadows and so on). The second model is the one used during the game proper. This is much simpler, because the software has to be able to animate the character very quickly in response to the game player's commands.

Rendering
For more on rendering, see page 138

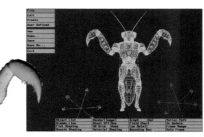

Wireframe Model

Finished Frame

OPENING SEQUENCE
This model of the fighting praying mantis used for the opening sequence of the game is complex and incorporates high-quality rendering. It takes the animator's computer hours to draw each frame.

ACTION MODELS
The model used in the game is much simpler than the one used for the introductory sequence. During the game, the software can draw the model in three ways, which range from least detailed and fastest to most detailed and slowest.

Simple Wireframe
This model has less than a third of the surfaces of the opening sequence model.

Quick Draw
The fastest way to draw the character is to fill every surface with flat color.

Better-looking
A slower way is smoothing each area of color to give a less blocky look.

Surface Patterns
The most sophisticated technique, and the slowest, adds surface patterns to the model.

PLAYING THE GAME
In the game, the software animates the two fighters and their 3-D surroundings, redrawing the whole scene up to 25 times every second.

Camera Angles
During the bout, the game changes the player's viewpoint. This also heightens the 3-D effect.

Faster but Cruder
To speed up the animation, the player can make the software use one of the simpler drawing techniques.

VIDEO COMPRESSION

Without compression there would only be enough space on a CD-ROM for approximately 20 seconds of broadcast-quality video. Furthermore, the speed at which an average CD-ROM drive transfers data means it would take about three seconds to display each frame. The only way to achieve an acceptable level of playback is to compress video files down to a practical size.

HOW COMPRESSION WORKS

Most video compression formats can be played back using Apple's *QuickTime* or Microsoft's *Video for Windows*. Once installed, these programs engage automatically whenever a CD-ROM contains digital video. The compression process is usually carried out by the software developer, with the user's computer simply decompressing the original image for playback. Although a great deal of processing power is needed for the compression stage, a relatively small amount is required for decompression.

In most cases, compression can remove 95 percent of the original data contained in an analog image. This is acceptable because most moving pictures contain information that can be removed without greatly affecting the overall image quality. Compression systems use complex mathematical codes called algorithms, which analyze a picture and discard surplus information.

VISUALIZING VIDEO

Broadcast television transmits 30 frames per second, and each video frame contains about one megabyte of data. This means it would take 180 CD-ROMs to hold an hour-long movie. But with compression, an hour-long movie fits on one CD-ROM.

IMAGE DISTORTION

Compression techniques are improving all the time, but it is still difficult to match the quality of broadcast television. Compression works best if the original video material is of high quality – but if the source material is poor the pictures suffer. Factors such as flashing lights, fast movement, or distortion on the original footage can confuse compression software and produce unwanted effects. A common problem, called pixelation or blocking, can sometimes be seen during fast-moving sequences. If a person suddenly starts to run, the compression system cannot keep up, and images may break up into tiny colored blocks.

DATA REDUCTION

Compression software uses a "key frame" to draw a video sequence, such as this one from Origin's *Wing Commander III*. Subsequent frames only contain data about the changes to the key frame, greatly reducing the amount of data needed for playback.

Key Frame
The opening image of a compressed video sequence contains all the data relating to the image.

Selected Data
Subsequent frames only contain data relating to the actor's new position, and the area he previously occupied. Data for the rest of the image is not needed.

The Result
The result is that subsequent frames can be drawn using a fraction of the data contained in the key frame.

MPEG COMPRESSION

The compression system currently causing the most excitement in the multimedia industry was developed by MPEG (Motion Picture Experts Group). It is very powerful, offering compression ratios of up to 200:1 – in other words, the compressed video files are just half a percent of their original size. There are two ways to play back MPEG-compressed video. One way is to use a special accelerator card or module containing hardware devoted to processing MPEG video. The other way is to use a software-only MPEG player, although this requires a powerful computer to achieve acceptable playback quality. The latest version, MPEG-2, works with digital video disc technology. It can improve the video capabilities of a multimedia computer enough to play high-quality motion pictures.

HARDWARE ASSISTANCE
MPEG video performance can be greatly improved with hardware acceleration. The card or module fits inside a computer or console and processes MPEG video at high speed.

PUTTING VIDEO INTO A TITLE

Authoring software
For more on authoring software, see page 116

The final stage in creating video for multimedia is to incorporate the video clips into a title, using authoring software. Developers have come up with various ways to hide the fact that most video clips play in small windows rather than taking up the full screen. One way is to blend the video clip into a larger image that acts as a border – the overall effect makes the video look bigger than it really is. Another technique is called pixel doubling. This takes the video data for one pixel and spreads it over four instead, creating a much larger image – but with less definition. Pixel doubling can turn video from quarter-screen to full-screen size, but only on more powerful computer systems. Some titles have optional "enlarge" buttons that will play larger video clips on more powerful systems, either by using pixel doubling, or by storing two different versions of the video file, one large, one small.

BLENDING
The video clips in Wienerworld's *Bob Dylan: Highway 61 Interactive* are integrated into a larger image to disguise their small size. In this scene, a video clip of an interview with Eric Clapton plays in a dressing-room mirror.

Pixels Up Close
This enlargement shows how pixel doubling spreads data for one pixel over a group of four.

PIXEL DOUBLING
Blown Away, by Imagination Pilots, uses pixel doubling to increase the apparent size of the video on the screen.

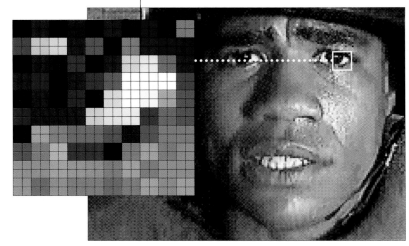

ENLARGING WINDOWS
Dorling Kindersley's *Eyewitness Encyclopedia of Nature* stores two different files for some video clips. On a sufficiently powerful system, users can click a button to watch the larger version.

MULTIMEDIA DOWN THE LINE

In the future, much of our multimedia may arrive down a telephone line rather than on a CD-ROM. This chapter explores the world of the information superhighway and the multimedia services it offers, from the Internet and the World Wide Web to on-line services and interactive television. It also takes a look into the future to see how multimedia may become part of everyone's daily lives.

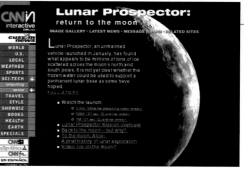

FINDING YOUR WAY

The interconnected nature of the World Wide Web is one of its greatest strengths, but to the novice, navigating a path through the hundreds of millions of documents stored on the Web, just to locate a single piece of information, can seem an impossible task. Fortunately the linked nature of the Web has made it relatively simple for companies to develop sophisticated "search engines." These act as vast databases of Web contents that users can use to search for the specific information they seek. The Web contains information on virtually every topic under the sun: this page gives but a small taste of what the Web has to offer.

KEEPING UP WITH NEWS

The flood of news on the Web is growing all the time, with most of the major broadcasting houses and newspapers now making their information available on-line. You can check your share prices, keep up with world events as they happen, or find out about the latest scientific discoveries.

Keyword Searches
You can search for specific information using keywords.

ON-LINE TRAINING AND EDUCATION

On-line training is a fast-growing area of the Web, and it is being explored by both educational institutions and commercial companies. Although CD-ROMs are very effective in providing distance education and training, on-line training has several important advantages. It provides students with the opportunity to interact with tutors and other students, using special "chat" sites or virtual conferences, and it offers access to a vast range of research resources.

On-line prospectus
This section of our Website outlines the Open University's teaching methods, the courses we offer, and the qualifications you can gain. For more detailed information please ask for one of our printed prospectuses, using the on-line request form. UK residents can get personal help and advice on study from one of our Regional Centres. In Continental Western Europe you can contact one of our local representatives.

CONTENTS
- Introduction to the OU
- Basic facts and figures
- How the Open University teaches
- Your study options
- Choosing courses
- How to become a student
- Fees and other costs
- Returning to study
- Credit transfer

Distance Learning
The UK's Open University has offered home-study degree courses for decades, supplying course material via the mail, TV, and radio. Some of its courses can now be studied on-line. E-mail, the Web, and live virtual seminars are used to deliver materials and hold tutorials.

THE SEARCH ENGINE

For most people a search engine is the essential Web tool. There are many to choose from, each offering a slightly different approach to finding information. Some include features for advanced searching using logical expressions; others provide Web directories; and some group their findings into similar types of sites, making it easier for the user to eliminate "matches" that are not of interest.

Directory Listings
To help in the hunt for information, some search engines provide directory-style listings of Web sites, organized into categories such as business, computing, entertainment, and so on.

Virtual Conferences
Scheduled live events with guest speakers take place via the Web, enabling hundreds, even thousands, of students to tune in from home and participate.

Aerial View

Asking Questions
Students ask questions by typing in this box. A moderator receives them via e-mail and relays them to the speaker.

Listening in
Students listen to the speaker using live audio feeds.

GOVERNMENT AND ORGANIZATIONS

Many government departments, charities, and non-profit-making organizations maintain a presence on the Web, using it as a means of promoting their work in front of a global audience, and enabling the public to access information about them at the click of a button. From the heads of state to the local charity, you can almost certainly find out where to contact them by looking on the Web.

Charities

Non-profit Organizations

Government Departments

Military Concerns

ELECTRONIC COMMERCE

The volume of commercial traffic on the Web is enormous, and increasing daily. You can do everything from purchasing software for your computer – which you can usually download on the spot – to banking or ordering the weekly shopping. Most commercial sites use sophisticated encryption techniques to protect and verify personal information, such as customers' credit-card details.

PC Banking
This Citibank site offers PC banking, enabling customers to manage their finances on-line.

Try Before You Buy
The Gap clothing store has an interactive Web site where customers can mix and match the season's styles before deciding what to buy.

On-line Shopping
Customers of this UK supermarket can register on-line. Once their credit-card details have been verified with a bank, they receive a unique Customer ID number which they use to make future purchases. Purchases are delivered direct to their home.

PURSUING INTERESTS

The Web has information on just about every sphere of human activity. Whether your interests include mainstream entertainments, such as music and sport, or something more obscure, you are likely to find fellow enthusiasts on the Web.

Travel
Travel sites may simply provide information on worldwide destinations, or enable you to book flights and hotels.

Sports and Leisure Activities

On-line Games and Entertainment

Pushy Products

With so many sources of information available on the Web, and the associated problems of locating what you want, "push" services are fast becoming the way to get information delivered direct to your desktop, without having to go in search of it. These services push information to you rather than waiting for you to "pull" it from the Web by following links. Many offer the opportunity to select in advance the topics of information that interest you, showing you only information related to those topics when you use the service.

POINTCAST NETWORK SERVICES

The PointCast Network allows you to select from topics such as news, industry, weather, sport, and health, for example, and then choose the source(s) from which you would prefer to receive information for each one. When you connect to the network, PointCast retrieves all the latest information from the Web.

DESKTOP CHANNELS

Microsoft's *Internet Explorer 4* offers a push service with its "channels." Accessed directly from the desktop, the channels bring information to you, without you having to go onto the Web.

International Content
The BBC provides information for one of the UK channels. Users in the US receive channels that are operated by American providers.

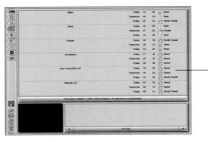

Up-to-the-minute Forecast
Among other things, PointCast enables users to monitor and compare weather conditions at specified locations worldwide.

Subscribing
Internet Explorer only updates information on the channels to which you subscribe.

MULTIMEDIA ON THE WEB

Although the World Wide Web grows more advanced every day, it doesn't yet compete with the compelling entertainment that a television, radio, or even a CD-ROM can provide. This is because the technology for sending large digital files across the Internet is still evolving and cannot yet match the data quality or transmission speeds of these other media. Many companies are working to change this by developing techniques for sending multimedia data, such as sound and video, smoothly and quickly over the Internet. Although these technologies are still in their infancy, the delivery of multimedia in real time over the Web is at last becoming a real possibility.

BIG FILES, SMALL PATH

Digital technology places many constraints on sending multimedia files over a network such as the Internet. Whereas analog data can be sent through the airwaves in almost infinite amounts, the size of digital files is limited by the capacities of the different cables, servers, and modems that transport them. Because most people access the Web using relatively slow Internet connections, it can take a long time to download large multimedia files. In the early days of the Web, users had to download these files to their computer before they could play them. Often this meant a wait of several minutes, or even hours, and the files usually occupied a considerable amount of disk space when they got there. But new technologies for transmitting digital data are being developed all the time, and while we wait for the promised broadband networks of the information superhighway to come into being, technologies such as "streaming" are doing much to make true multimedia experiences on the Web a reality.

STREAMING DATA DOWN THE LINE

Streaming is a continuous-delivery technology that is dramatically improving the performance of multimedia on the Web. It enables users to view or listen to a file in real time, while it is being transferred to their computer, getting round the problem of lengthy file download times. Although streaming technology is developing fast, it is still more difficult to stream video data than sound data. This is mainly because video files are more complex than sound files: the quality issues are more demanding and technical limitations harder to overcome. It also requires a more powerful computer to decompress video data "on the fly" than audio data. But as compression techniques gradually improve, reducing the size of the files to be transferred, lengthier and better quality video and sound files will become available on the Web.

(1) Data Stream Starts
As soon as it is requested, the video file is divided into small packets and sent over the Internet to the destination computer.

HOW STREAMING WORKS
This illustration explains how a multimedia file can be streamed over the Internet so that it can be played within seconds of the user requesting it from his or her Web browser. The example shown here is a video file, but the principles apply equally to audio, animation, or other large multimedia files being transmitted over the Internet.

(2) Download Begins
The first packets of data arrive at the destination and are downloaded into a "buffer," a temporary area of the computer's memory.

(3) Buffer Fills Up
As more data arrives, the buffer fills up. Once it is full, the video starts to play. This process usually takes just a few seconds.

Display Panel
This panel displays information about the data stream, such as how long you may expect to wait before the file starts playing, and the rate of data transmission.

(4) Playback Begins
As the first part of the video starts to play, the next part is being downloaded into the buffer, ready to play when the first one finishes. This continuous stream of data, from Web to buffer to player, continues seamlessly in the background until the clip ends.

MAKING IT HAPPEN

The technology for sending digital data over the Internet is constantly improving, but the sheer variety of multimedia file formats available, combined with the different Web browsers and computers used to view them, creates its own set of constraints. A sound file created on a Macintosh, for example, may not be readily understood by a Web browser on a PC. Few Web browsers can handle by default every type of multimedia file that exists on the Web. They can automatically display elements such as text, graphics, and simple animated files, but most require the aid of additional "plug-in" software to handle more sophisticated or unusual files. These applications are fine-tuned for the individual requirements of different files, and extend the multimedia potential of Web browsers. The latest browsers bring exciting multimedia closer still, with features that enable them to play complete programs over the Web, without the use of plug-ins. These programs, known as "applets" or "controls," are created using programming systems, such as Java and Microsoft's ActiveX, that are designed for use on the Internet.

PLUG-IN SOFTWARE

Plug-in applications work in conjunction with Web browser programs, giving them additional functions. Many use compression algorithms to encode multimedia files into small, manageable formats that can be sent easily over the Internet. Some, like the *RealPlayer* audio and video plug-in from Real Networks, use streaming technology and have special features for handling the unpredictable nature of Internet connections – including the ability to detect which bandwidth is most suitable at a given time. When the data arrives at the destination computer, plug-ins decompress and decode it so that the file appears perfectly normal when played back. Most plug-ins can be downloaded from the Web on demand.

Compression
Fore more on compression, see page 156

Interactive Pages
This page on the Gap site was created using Macromedia's Shockwave plug-in. Shockwave uses compression and streaming technologies to make files created in Director suitable for use on the Web.

EMBEDDED MULTIMEDIA

Multimedia has its most immediate impact on the Web when the user does not have to spend time downloading extra software to make it work. Java applets and ActiveX controls can be embedded into Web pages and run automatically by most of today's Web browsers. They enable Web pages to provide almost limitless functions, ranging from on-line games to database integration. Animated files provide another immediate form of multimedia on the Web, and have the advantage of requiring no special programming skills.

Animated File Formats
Most Web browsers can handle "animated .gif" files by default. These files contain a series of images that the browser plays in succession to give the appearance of movement.

Applets and Controls
The latest Web browsers can run Java applets, such as this Web Invaders game, and ActiveX controls on a Web page, without the need for additional plug-in software.

MULTIMEDIA PLUG-INS

With suitable plug-ins installed, Web browsers can handle all manner of multimedia, from virtual worlds to interactive animations or live audio and video feeds. Because of the different requirements of each file type, different plug-ins are usually needed to handle each one.

Virtual Worlds
This Superscape page was created using a VRML (Virtual Reality Modeling Language) plug-in.

Freedom of Movement
Virtual worlds enable users to move about freely. Here, you can go from inside to outside, or even take a swim, using the direction buttons to change your orientation.

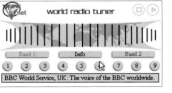

Virtual Style
By dragging this button up or down you can create a series of virtual outfits.

Live Radio
This Virgin Net page relays live radio broadcasts over the Web. It uses the RealPlayer plug-in from Real Networks to stream data across the Internet.

ON-LINE SERVICES

While the Internet grew up without any real parents, privately run on-line services were set up by organizations as commercial concerns. Subscribers pay a fee to access an on-line service, so the service must have an extra something that is not available on the Internet. For many people, this is the clearly categorized, well-sign posted content, the user-friendly interface that enables quick and easy access to information, and member support. Such features are especially attractive to beginners. On-line services also carry a wide range of useful databases that are often unavailable on the Internet. These may include encyclopedias, airline and train timetables, and press clippings. In addition, most private services now offer full integration with the Internet, providing a gateway to the World Wide Web.

THE PIONEERS

In the 1970s, after communication over a telephone line and modem became possible, commercial organizations realized that they could offer a public information service on-line. One of the first companies to attempt this was the state-owned France Telecom, which set up its *Minitel* service in 1982. In a bold move aimed at upgrading France's technological culture, the company gave every phone subscriber in the country a free terminal, making France one of the first on-line communities.

Soon after that, the first American service took off. *CompuServe* was originally the data-processing department of an insurance company, but in the early 1980s it started using its spare computing capacity to offer services to personal computer users. Since then it has expanded beyond recognition and been joined by other services, such as *America Online*. Many smaller services also enjoyed a brief life: *Prodigy* (belonging to IBM and Sears), *GEnie* (General Electric), *Delphi* (The News Corporation), and Apple's *eWorld*. In 1995, Microsoft launched its own service, *The Microsoft Network*. All of these services offer a similar mix of products, although the level of Internet access and degree of internationalism vary.

Minitel

In the early 1980s, France Telecom's *Minitel* was providing an on-line telephone directory, as well as a route through which companies could advertise or provide information: there are now 24,000 such information providers.

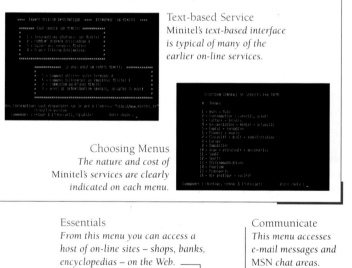

Text-based Service
Minitel's *text-based interface is typical of many of the earlier on-line services.*

Choosing Menus
The nature and cost of Minitel's services are clearly indicated on each menu.

EWORLD
Apple Computer's *eWorld* was launched in 1994. The simple graphical organization of information was typified by the "town square" interface used on the opening screen. Each of the buildings led to a range of services.

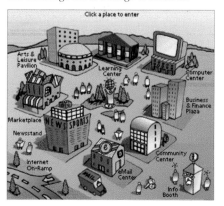

THE MICROSOFT NETWORK (MSN)
MSN was first launched in 1995 and distributed with Windows 95 software. In 1996, *MSN* underwent a radical face-lift, adopting the analogy of TV station with different channels. It now schedules events as well as providing reference and educational products, such as encyclopedias and interactive games.

MSN Show on Channel 4

Essentials
From this menu you can access a host of on-line sites – shops, banks, encyclopedias – on the Web.

Communicate
This menu accesses e-mail messages and MSN chat areas.

Channels
These buttons access MSN's "channels." Each channel has a theme, such as lifestyle or news.

WHAT THEY OFFER

On-line services offer structure and content in a traditionally chaotic environment. They provide custom-made software with clear, user-friendly interfaces that subscribers use to access a service's up-to-date information. All on-line services offer e-mail and most also offer reference tools, virtual shopping, games, and news. News comes in on a regular basis from major news providers and may even be tailored for specific countries. Highly organized and maintained forums run by outside organizations and experts are also common. Forums contain information about a particular subject; have bulletin board-style areas for visitors to post messages to each other; and often provide a set of related resources, such as contacts, tips, or software. Many on-line services also have informal discussion areas, or "chat rooms," where anyone can join in with the conversation using their keyboard. Although on-line services have relatively few forums each, they are considered by many to be better organized and more friendly than their Internet equivalents.

HOW AN ON-LINE SERVICE WORKS

CompuServe is an on-line service used around the world. Since 1995, *CompuServe* has also provided access to the Internet and its many newsgroups, file transfer sites, and the World Wide Web. Members access its services by clicking buttons on the main window or the toolbar.

Toolbar
The toolbar appears on every CompuServe screen. Users can customize it to provide short-cuts to their favorite areas.

Finding Your Way
Search CompuServe or go directly to a specific area.

E-mail

Personal Information
This button opens the "filing cabinet" where text, mail messages, and any other files can be stored for reading or printing off-line (when disconnected from the service).

Getting Help
This area shows how to use CompuServe's different services.

Member Forums
CompuServe *has a variety of forums where members can join in with live discussions.*

Contents
From the Table of Contents icon, members can access CompuServe's main content – including news, on-line shopping, and education areas – quickly and simply.

On-line News
This service offers up-to-the-minute information from news services such as the Press Association.

Shopping Services
If you know where to look, you can shop on the Internet, but on-line services make things easy by providing "electronic malls."

Search an Encyclopedia
On-line reference works such as The Hutchinson Encyclopedia can be searched for pictures or text.

View Before Buying
By accessing the Interflora "store," you can choose your flowers from the pictures and descriptions provided. You then simply enter the relevant billing, payment, and delivery information.

Downloading Images
After you have searched for and found the image you want (in this case Greta Garbo) you can view it and then save it on your hard disk.

INTERACTIVE TELEVISION

INTERACTIVE TELEVISION is a term used to describe the merging of computer and television technologies into a single entity. In the near future, we will be able to use the television to watch scheduled programs, select videos to watch on-line, order the weekly shopping, play games with friends in other countries, or pay our bills. The technology needed to provide such services already exists, but in order to justify the vast financial investment needed to connect every home to a broadband network, service providers must first find out whether there is a demand for the services they offer. Around the world, service providers are using pilot programs to try out their systems and discover which features are most popular, and which will be the "killer applications" that customers are prepared to pay for.

VIDEO-ON-DEMAND

The arrival of the VCR in the 1970s meant it was possible for the first time to watch a movie whenever you chose. But you first had to tape it or rent it. Video-on-demand, however, provides the movie instantaneously. Using a remote control supplied by the service provider, you choose a movie category, such as drama, comedy, or action. An "electronic rental store" then presents an extensive list of movies in that category. With the press of a button, you select one, and seconds later it appears on the screen. You can then stop it, pause it, rewind or fast-forward it, just as though it were a video in a VCR machine. Many commentators believe that video-on-demand will be the killer application of interactive televison.

NEAR VIDEO-ON-DEMAND

A cheaper alternative to video-on-demand, known as "near video-on-demand," has been adopted by some satellite television services. It is a development of the "pay-per-view" systems already widespread on cable television. The movies it offers each start every 15 or 30 minutes. After selecting a movie you are then told how long to wait before it starts to play.

Satellite
For more on satellites, see page 161

REMOTE CONTROL
BT's interactive television service is controlled by a multipurpose remote control unit.

Direction Button
This gamepad-style button enables you to navigate through options and menus.

OK Button
This unit has an OK button for making selections.

Function Buttons
These buttons enable you to select different options on the screen.

Video Controls
Video-on-demand can be paused, rewound, or fast-forwarded at will.

List of Movies

MOVIE CHOICE
Customers of Time Warner Cable's Full Services Network in Orlando, Florida can choose from an extensive list of popular movies.

HOME SHOPPING

Many people have experienced a form of home shopping through mail-order catalogs or television shopping channels, but these services can offer only a limited range of goods. The home shopping service offered on interactive television systems is far more flexible. Viewers can enter virtual stores and examine goods by revolving them in three dimensions on the screen. They can read the details on a product's packaging, and make a purchase simply by pressing a button on their handset. This debits their credit card, and the goods are then delivered to the home.

GAMES AND NEWS-ON-DEMAND

Most interactive television trials are offering games to their customers. These games are sent to the set-top box in the same way as video-on-demand. They can then be played either alone or with friends. Another option is to play against someone else linked up to the network: once the player has selected a game, he or she can compete against other opponents who are playing at the same time.

Games
For more on games, see page 44

Another significant service is news-on-demand. Instead of watching news bulletins when they are scheduled by a broadcast television company, users of interactive television can call up the latest bulletin from major news networks, such as CNN, at any time. A sports-on-demand service is also possible. This system can be applied to any category of television program, and could theoretically do away with the entire concept of television schedules.

Virtual Supermarket
Time Warner Cable's ShopperVision shows a 3-D graphic view of the products on the shelves.

Set-top Box
Most interactive television systems use a set-top box to decode the signals that are transmitted to the home.

SERVICES ON TRIAL
Both the Time Warner Cable trial in the United States and the BT trial in the UK are experimenting with a wide range of services such as video-on-demand, home shopping, and on-line games.

Graphical Interface
The Time Warner Cable trial uses an interface called Carousel, a revolving visual display of the services available to the viewer.

Main Menu
Participants in the BT pilot program are presented with a main menu in the form of numbered icons.

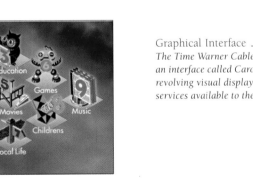

Video Games
Time Warner Cable offers a range of 64-bit action games with three-dimensional color images and CD-quality sound.

HOW INTERACTIVE TELEVISION WORKS

Participants in interactive television pilot programs, enjoying the range of services available, may not appreciate the technical difficulties in bringing these services to the home. Unlike broadcast television, an interactive service allows the customer to decide which service to use at any given time. Therefore, not only does the service provider have to manage the task of sending massive amounts of digital data over a cable, but it must also set up a system for receiving signals back from the customer. For example, if a customer decides to watch a movie, he or she chooses it from an on-screen list, using the remote control. This signal then travels to a computer in the operations center, where it is interpreted and acted upon. The right movie is located, and sent back to the appropriate home. All this takes place in less than a second, and there may be thousands of similar requests every minute, presenting the service provider with an enormous technical challenge.

Optical Fiber

Fiber-optic cable is made up of fibers of extraordinarily pure glass. Instead of transmitting data in electrical impulses as copper wires do, the glass fibers transmit it in pulses of light. Traveling at great speed, these are internally reflected throughout their journey from one end of the cable to the other.

PROVIDING AN INTERACTIVE SERVICE

Providing an interactive television service is an impressive feat of modern engineering. Different pilot programs use different techniques. The example shown here – supplying video-on-demand – is based on Time Warner Cable's Full Service Network program in Orlando, Florida.

(1) Operations Center
The operations center is the nerve center of an interactive TV service. It receives requests from customers, locates the relevant material, and sends the digital data back to the customer's home.

(2) Storage Vaults
Data such as digital video is held in compressed form in large storage devices called vaults. A typical vault houses up to 100 magnetic hard drives – enough to store more than 500 movies.

(3) Digital Server
The server is a powerful computer that acts as the central brains of the system. When it receives a request, it locates the correct movie and divides the data into packets; it then adds the address of the destination to each one, and sends them to the ATM switch.

(6) Fiber-optic Cable
The digital data is transmitted from the operations center to the neighborhood node along a fiber-optic cable.

(4) ATM Switch
ATM (Asynchronous Transfer Mode) is an advanced version of the packet switching used by the Internet. The ATM switch sends the packets of data coming from the server to the modulator at great speed.

(5) Modulator
The modulator places the information it receives at the correct frequency for transmission through the network. This signal is then sent to the neighborhood node.

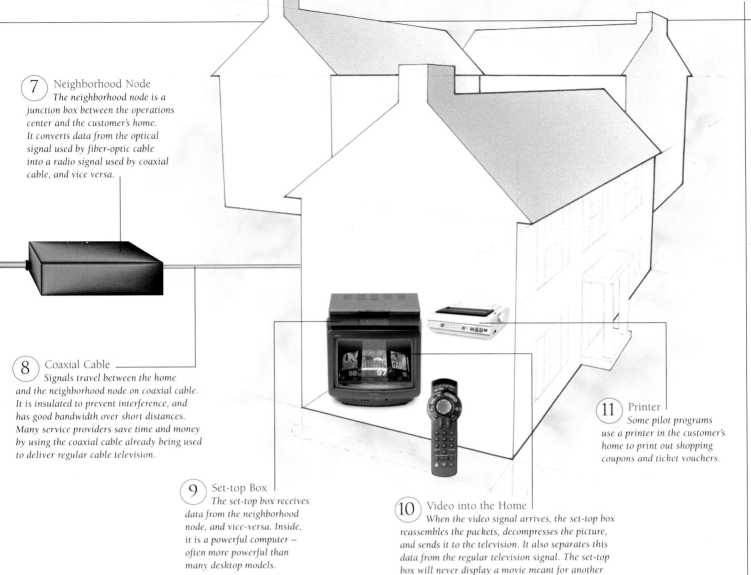

7 Neighborhood Node
*The neighborhood node is a
junction box between the operations
center and the customer's home.
It converts data from the optical
signal used by fiber-optic cable
into a radio signal used by coaxial
cable, and vice versa.*

8 Coaxial Cable
*Signals travel between the home
and the neighborhood node on coaxial cable.
It is insulated to prevent interference, and
has good bandwidth over short distances.
Many service providers save time and money
by using the coaxial cable already being used
to deliver regular cable television.*

9 Set-top Box
*The set-top box receives
data from the neighborhood
node, and vice-versa. Inside,
it is a powerful computer –
often more powerful than
many desktop models.*

10 Video into the Home
*When the video signal arrives, the set-top box
reassembles the packets, decompresses the picture,
and sends it to the television. It also separates this
data from the regular television signal. The set-top
box will never display a movie meant for another
house because it reads the address on the packets,
and will not decode data addressed to another house.*

11 Printer
*Some pilot programs
use a printer in the customer's
home to print out shopping
coupons and ticket vouchers.*

Digital Production Center

Before movies or television programs are sent for
storage at the operations center, they have to be
compressed, so that they will occupy as little storage
space and bandwidth as possible. This compression
is carried out by powerful computers at a digital
production center, often located away from the main
operations center. The production center also creates
items such as logos, animated promotional sequences,
and the visual interface from which the customer
navigates the interactive television service.

Animation Suite
*The production center houses
a digital animation suite for
creating animated sequences
and for 3-D modeling. It uses
powerful workstations, such
as the Silicon Graphics Indigo
2 Extreme system shown here.*

INTO THE FUTURE

THE FUTURE FOR MULTIMEDIA looks dynamic: the quantity of digital information in our lives is ready to increase substantially over the next few decades, and it will improve dramatically in quality. Multimedia is evolving rapidly and in unexpected ways, but the broad trends all point toward a convergence of today's new technologies: CD-ROM, the Internet, and interactive television. This convergence is at the heart of a much broader revolution, which not only affects the way information is packaged and how we interact with it, but also looks ready to transform the way we communicate with one another. Multimedia is now becoming both personal and portable, as these technologies demonstrate.

PERSONAL MULTIMEDIA

The multimedia that we receive on CD-ROM is mass-produced, and sites on the World Wide Web are open to a mass audience, but current trends are all toward making multimedia more personal. Videophones, multimedia e-mail, and videoconferencing are bringing personal multimedia into one-to-one communication. Portable computers now make it possible to play multimedia titles and access the Internet while on the move. And PDAs (Personal Digital Assistants), the handheld electronic pocketbooks that started out as simple digital diaries, are fast becoming wireless communication stations. At the same time, the computer industry is working to remedy the problem that after 25 years of extremely rapid technological progress, computers are still impersonal objects that many people find hard to use. The move toward computer recognition of handwriting and speech and toward new computer interfaces suggests that the future of multimedia is to be a lot more human.

Video Screen ———

Miniature Camera

VIDEOPHONE
This videophone can send medium-quality black-and-white video pictures over an ordinary telephone line. It also acts as a standard voice telephone.

FACE-TO-FACE COMMUNICATION

Multimedia messages can already be sent by computer users linked to a broadband network. In Berlin, where a fiber-optic ring has been installed, city architects can send their colleagues in the traffic department e-mail that might include a text message, a plan of a bridge to be repaired, and a video clip showing the volume of traffic at the bridge at rush hour. Also in the workplace, videoconferencing is enabling companies to set up international meetings without the expense or delay of travel. The other prime site for videoconferencing is in remote areas, where schools and medical centers can benefit from remote lessons and long-distance diagnosis. Videophones for the home, however, are proving slow to catch on. Research shows that, while family and friends may enjoy seeing some sort of image of each other while they talk, the small picture does not break the ice between strangers.

VIDEOCONFERENCING
Broadband computer networks and digital cameras enable long-distance business meetings to take place in videoconference rooms (above left) and ordinary office environments.

MULTIMEDIA IN YOUR HAND

PDAs can now combine the functions of a personal organizer, computer, Internet terminal, and mobile telephone all in one package, and they are rapidly changing the ways we access information. PDAs use a miniature keyboard or some form of data entry tablet, often with handwriting recognition. Just recently, mobile telephone manufacturers such as Nokia have started adding handheld computers to their phones to make hybrid systems, such as the Nokia 9000, that can communicate through wireless networks. At present most PDAs offer small, mono screens, but companies such as Cambridge Display Technology are already developing lightweight color displays that will enable developers to produce true multimedia PDAs within the next few years. As PDAs get smaller and more sophisticated, they will be able to provide us with information wherever we go, and we will be able to access that information on display devices as compact and diverse as a wristwatch or a display panel on the dashboard of a car.

PERSONAL DIGITAL ASSISTANT

Sony's Magic Link PDA combines the functions of an electronic diary with wireless e-mail and fax communications. It is based on the easy-to-use Magic Cap interface, which extends the "computer desktop" idea to its logical conclusion.

Screen
The user operates the PDA by pressing on the touch-sensitive screen with a plastic stylus.

Hallway
Activities outside the office are represented by doors to different rooms.

Downtown
Commercial services are represented by main-street buildings.

Desktop
The desk screen closely resembles an actual office or study.

On-screen Keyboard
The user types in messages by tapping an on-screen keyboard. Handwriting recognition is available as an optional extra.

HYBRID SYSTEM

The Nokia 9000 is a hybrid PDA that offers access to the Internet, via a keyboard and screen, and also acts as a mobile telephone. Its makers have had to sacrifice the quality of the display to keep its size and weight down, and the clam-shell design makes it awkward to use the telephone and computer at the same time.

Mobile Telephone
When the case is closed, the Nokia 9000 functions as a telephone.

Portable Computer
When the case is open, the Nokia 9000 becomes a miniature computer, offering access to the Internet and allowing users to send e-mail and browse pages from the World Wide Web.

FLEXIBLE DISPLAYS

This prototype television screen, developed by Cambridge Display Technology and Seiko-Epson, offers a glimpse of the future of personal multimedia devices. Made from light-emitting plastic (LEP), it is flexible and lightweight, with a thickness of just 2 mm. Although it is monochrome, color LEP displays are already being developed, and it will not be long before such technology is changing the face of PDAs.

High-resolution Screen
The screen has a high resolution and can display full television pictures.

THE FUTURE: DIGITAL PAPER?

In his science-fiction novel *The Diamond Age* writer Neal Stephenson described what he called "digital paper." Although digital paper looks and feels like ordinary paper, it is in fact made up of millions of microscopic nanocomputers. Each one can communicate with a worldwide data network; change its color so that the sheet as a whole can display pictures; or vibrate so that the whole sheet can act as a speaker, making it the ultimate multimedia display. Digital paper can even interact with the user: it can recognize your handwriting and understand what you say, and it can be folded up and put in your pocket when not in use. Although this idea may seem an impossibility, most of the key technologies that would be needed for digital paper are already visible on the technological horizon.

THE HOME OF THE FUTURE

Predicting the future is a dangerous business – just think of all those 1950s comic strips that had us buzzing around in hover cars and spending our vacations on the moon. Such predictions have yet to come true, but by examining the technological developments we have seen in recent years, it is possible to paint a credible picture of the multimedia services that will be available to an ordinary home in, say, 2010. Naturally, we cannot say for certain that all homes will resemble our scenario; but we can say that there is no technological reason why they cannot be like this. A characteristic feature of the new services will almost certainly be their transformation of certain activities, such as shopping and attending conferences, that have always involved travel: in the future, on-line and virtual reality equipment will probably give us the option of pursuing much of our business without stirring from our home.

CONVERGENCE

The future will bring a convergence of different technologies, particularly of television, the telephone, and the computer. At present, the three remain physically separate in interactive television pilot programs and need to be connected by a cable – but this is changing: several companies have combined a television with a computer. Some of these machines, such as the Fujitsu/ICL PCTV, have full double function, changing from television to computer at the press of a button; others are predominantly computers that provide a television "window" on-screen.

PCTV
For more on the PCTV, see page 163

VIRTUAL REALITY IN THE HOME

Within a few years, virtual reality computer games for the home are likely to be in general use. As personal computers and games consoles become more powerful, they will be able to generate a quality of image comparable to that found in today's virtual reality arcade machines. Initially, these games will be supplied on compact discs, but before long they will be generally available on-line on the Internet. Technically, this is already possible: a virtual reality game can be downloaded just like any other file – but virtual reality programs use up such an immense amount of data that few people would bother to download them without a high-speed broadband connection. Once they become easy to download, however, Arthur C. Clarke, the science fiction writer, predicts that virtual reality will "eat television alive." Many observers agree.

MULTIMEDIA HOUSE
From the outside, the home of the future will probably not look very different from a typical home of today. But on the inside, we will have access to many new services. To illustrate this, each room of the house below contains a member of the family engaged in a different multimedia activity, explained in more detail on this and the next page.

Teleworking
Anna is in her office taking part in a virtual conference.

On-line Information
Lydia is using a computer linked to an on-line database to help her with her homework.

Virtual Reality Game
Ben is playing a virtual reality game in his room.

Multimedia Newspaper
Uncle Oscar is reading a personalized multimedia newspaper in the kitchen.

Interactive Television
Nick is in the living room shopping while watching an interactive movie.

INTERACTIVE TELEVISION SERVICES
In the living room, Nick, father of the family, is watching an interactive film while doing the shopping. He does this on a very large screen that hangs like a painting on the wall.
Most of the screen shows a mountain with a climber on it. A question is displayed: "Do you want to take the North Col route or go straight up the West face?" But Nick has put the movie on hold, and is concentrating on his shopping.

Interactive Movie
The video-on-demand service that Nick subscribes to holds over 25,000 movies, from old black-and-white classics to the latest interactive blockbusters.

On-line Shopping
A window on the screen shows a range of olive oil bottles, each labeled with price, origin, and dietary information. Nick selects one with the handset, and a voice says: "You have selected one quart of Oliva. The price is ten dollars. This amount has been debited from your account. Thank you."

Remote Control
Nick uses the remote control to choose items on the screen, as well as to regulate other devices in the room, such as the air-conditioning.

"Flat Screen" Shopping
Nick could have gone to a virtual supermarket, where he can walk up and the down the aisle as in a real store, but he finds this "flat screen" shopping less of a strain. He does not like virtual reality, saying it gives him a headache.

Virtual Conference
When she first took part in a virtual conference, Anna found the experience strange – not least because she could put her hand straight through her colleagues. But she is now used to it.

Broadband Network
Anna's computer is linked directly into a fiber-optic broadband network, with enough bandwidth to handle her virtual conference.

HOME OFFICE
In her office, Anna, the mother of the family, is involved in a virtual conference with her colleagues in Paris and Tokyo. She wears a pair of virtual reality glasses, connected by infrared link to her computer. Through her headset she sees a virtual meeting with several people sitting around a table. Disembodied hands pass around documents, which are then stored on her computer. The faces and bodies are realistic, but not yet perfect likenesses.

Infrared Link
An infrared link connects Anna's keyboard to her computer. She uses the keyboard to control the documents that appear on her screen and to call up her own files.

SMART APPLIANCES

The house of the multimedia future will be "smart" – most devices will probably be interconnected, and controlled and coordinated by a central computer. This means that the toaster will automatically switch on a certain number of minutes after the electric toothbrush has been switched off, and the washing machine will diagnose its own faults and automatically call the service engineer. Although all this is not strictly multimedia, it will be a direct consequence of technology that has been established as a result of the multimedia revolution. Furthermore, the social changes implicit in this new technology will be far-reaching. Governments, businesses, and the general public will be faced with many more choices – and with some perplexing questions.

FREEDOM OF INFORMATION

The arrival of the photocopier in the 1970s made it simple to produce copies of printed information for distribution. Today, a similar phenomenon is taking place on the Internet. Anyone with a computer and a modem can tap into the Internet and access and publish vast quantities of information – and there is little a government or regulatory body can do to prevent it. No one can yet say whether this total freedom of access to information is a good thing or not, and the issue is likely to remain controversial for years to come.

Internet
For more on the Internet, see page 164

Portable Screen
Oscar's screen is linked to the house's controlling computer by a radio link. The screen can be moved anywhere in the house and will still display images. It can even be taken outside, although the signal starts to fade at the bottom of the garden.

Controlling Computer

Underneath the stairs in the home of the future is a powerful computer. Although hidden from sight, it acts as the central nervous system of the house. Its functions range from sending out video signals to the various screens in the home to controlling the temperature and humidity in each room.

Communication Links
The controlling computer can communicate in several ways. It is linked directly to the information superhighway by fiber-optic cable. It is also linked to the other computers in the house by coaxial cable, and to many of the smaller appliances via radio signals and infrared links.

INTELLIGENT SEARCHER

Each member of the family has a personalized newspaper (it is still called this, even though most people no longer print it out). The newspaper is multimedia – a mix of text, still pictures, video, and sound. It was created by an automatic "intelligent searcher" – a program that looks through hundreds of electronic newspapers, assembling what it believes to be the most suitable collection of stories for each member of the family.

Personalized Newspaper
In the kitchen, Uncle Oscar is reading his newspaper on a portable screen placed on the breakfast counter. He has asked the intelligent searcher to look for football, traffic, and general political news, as well as a randomly generated selection of stories. At present, the screen is displaying a clip of last night's football game, while an article runs alongside it giving the sportscaster's opinion. Oscar's nephew, Ben, prefers to look at baseball reports, the computer games pages, and his favorite cartoons.

On-line Database
While doing her homework, Lydia has been distracted by news of an earthquake in Eastern Europe, so she is downloading video clips of it, and comparing the damage with that caused by other earthquakes. The clips are stored on a central educational database to which her school subscribes.

INTERACTIVE EDUCATION

In her bedroom, Lydia, age 10, is doing her homework, learning Spanish. She watches an episode of a Spanish soap opera; it stops regularly and asks her questions to test her comprehension. She speaks the answer out loud, and is immediately told if she is right. If she makes a mistake, an electronic "tutor," a cartoon character, appears on the screen to tell her what she has done wrong. If she needs to look up a word, she calls up the on-line dictionary; and if she is completely baffled, she can dial up her teacher at home and be given help via a videophone link.

SERIOUS QUESTIONS

What will all these multimedia services mean for people who enjoy going out to shop, simply for a change of scene or because it is their only chance to meet people? What will they do if the shopping streets and malls have closed down through lack of demand? And what will the people who used to work in those shops do then? How will white-collar workers, who were used to meeting and working with colleagues at the workplace, feel when teleworking (or telecommuting) enables them to do the same job in physical isolation at home? Will the freedom from the hassle of commuting compensate enough for the loss of social interaction that most of us take for granted today?

EMPTY CITIES

The idea of teleworking also raises concerns about the future of our cities. What will happen to cities – already suffering from the exodus of middle-class residents – when, as a result of teleworking, the office blocks become deserted because their former inhabitants are now working from home? These are critical questions, which show that great technological changes such as the multimedia revolution cannot meaningfully be considered in isolation but must also be seen in the light of their probable social and political consequences.

Headset
Mass-produced virtual reality headsets are becoming more common in people's homes.

Controller
Depending on which game is being played, the controller can represent a lance, a light saber, or a sword.

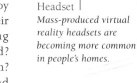

VIRTUAL REALITY GAMES

In his bedroom, 12-year-old Ben is wearing virtual reality gear. He is holding a stick, which he is prodding toward the window. In his virtual world he is a medieval knight, jousting (the stick is his lance). He is taking part in a global *Knights of the Round Table* tournament. Ben has gotten through to the fifth round, but since there are a million entrants his chances of winning the tournament (and the hand of the king's daughter) are remote.

Remote Opponent
Ben's opponent is another child, who wanted to play at the same time and has, the computer says, about the same level of skill as Ben. The child lives on the other side of the world.

GLOSSARY

A

Accelerator Card
A card that slots into a computer or console to speed up activities such as video playback or graphics drawing.

ActiveX Control
Similar to an applet, but created using Microsoft's ActiveX system rather than Java.

ADSL
An abbreviation for Asymmetric Digital Subscriber Line. An ADSL can transmit digital data in large quantities over existing telephone lines. It provides a wider and faster stream of data into the home than out of it.

Analog
A method of storing information as varying electrical voltages, rather than electronic code. Today's television sets, video recorders, radios, and telephones are analog devices.

Animation
The display of a sequence of still images to give the illusion of continuous motion.

Antialiasing
A technique used to reduce the jagged edges that appear around text and graphics when displayed on a screen; antialiasing blends the edge of every letter and image into its surroundings.

Applet
A small program, written in the Java programming language, that can be embedded into a Web page and activated from a Web browser. An applet may comprise a miniature animation, or interactive element, such as a game or spreadsheet.

Authoring
The process of combining various elements, such as text, sound, video, and animation, to produce a multimedia title.

Authoring Software
A computer program that links the different parts of a multimedia title together.

B

Binary
A counting system based on only two digits, 1 and 0. Computers store and manipulate all data and information in binary code.

Bit
Short for binary digit, a it is the smallest unit of information a computer can understand. Eight bits make a byte.

Broadband Network
A high-speed, high-capacity digital network that is gradually replacing conventional analog telephone networks. The information superhighway will be a broadband network.

Bus
A pathway of thin metallic tracks along which data travels to different parts of a computer. A PC contains several different buses and each connects different parts of the computer.

Byte
A unit of measure for binary data. Equivalent to eight bits.

C

Cartridge
A removable storage device that plugs into a games console.

Cartridges

CAD (Computer-Aided Design)
Computer programs for designing objects, usually in the fields of engineering, product design, and architecture.

CD-ROM
The abbreviation for Compact Disc Read-Only Memory. Often used for multimedia titles, CD-ROMs can store large amounts of data that can be read by a computer; an entire encyclopedia can be stored on one disc.

CD-ROM Drive
A piece of hardware that uses a laser to read data stored on a CD-ROM. This data can then be interpreted and played by a computer.

Cel
Part of an animation sequence where individual drawings are made on transparent plastic sheets, each one recording a different position of a moving object. They are then photographed by a camera.

Expansion Card

Chip
A tiny piece of silicon with miniature circuits imprinted on it. Chips are often used as a CPU or as memory.

Click
To press and immediately release a mouse button. To click on something is to position the pointer above it and then click.

Clock Speed
This refers to the speed at which the computer's CPU operates, normally given in megahertz. The higher the clock speed of the computer, the faster it can process information.

Command
An instruction that a user gives to the computer, such as to print a document.

Compression
A technique that reduces the size of computer files, so that, for example, more of them will fit onto a CD-ROM.

Console
A type of computer that plugs directly into a television set and is used mainly for playing games. The Sony PlayStation and the Sega Saturn are examples of consoles.

Convergence
A word used to describe the growing tendency of the new technologies to merge, such as by combining a computer with a television.

CPU (Central Processing Unit)
The main chip in a computer that interprets commands and instructions.

D

Data
Information that is stored in a digital form that computers can interpret.

Database
A database is simply a collection of related pieces of information, such as a list of addresses. The easiest way to think of a database is as a set of records stored in computerized form, much like a set of electronic index cards.

Data Transfer Rate
The amount of data that can be read from a hard disk or CD-ROM, usually expressed in kilobytes per second.

Desktop Publishing
A software program that lets you arrange a document's text and pictures on-screen. It can be used for laying out the pages of a magazine or a book.

Digital
Information that is stored as numbers (using the digits 0 and 1), as opposed to analog information. All data on a CD-ROM is stored in digital form whether it is sound, text, or video.

Digital TV
A system for sending digital rather than analog signals to a television set via satellite, terrestrial broadcast, or cable. These signals are received by a set-top box, which decodes them for display on a television screen.

Digitize
To convert information into digital form. For example, scanners are used to digitize pictures, and sound is digitized by a process called sampling.

Download
To transfer files to your computer from another computer via a modem. The opposite term is upload.

DVD
The abbreviation for Digital Video Disc, a DVD is a high-density compact disc format that can store over 14 times as much as data as the original CD-ROM.

E

Edutainment
Used to describe educational multimedia titles that combine education with entertainment.

E-mail (Electronic Mail)
Documents and messages you can send or receive directly on your computer.

Expansion Card
A card that sits inside a computer and adds extra capabilities, such as high-quality sound.

Expansion Slot
A slot inside a computer where you can insert an expansion card.

F

Fiber-optic Cable
A type of cable consisting of very thin strands of glass. It carries enormous amounts of information in the form of light pulses.

File
A grouping of information, such as a document or program, normally stored on a disk, that can be read by a computer.

Frame
Multimedia animation and video consists of a series of frames or pictures, as many as 25 frames every second.

G

Game Editor
Software used to build graphical environments for multimedia games.

Gigabyte
Equivalent to roughly a thousand megabytes.

Graphics
Pictorial information that is displayed on a computer screen.

Graphics Engine
Games software that can draw rooms and other objects from any angle to give the illusion of a three-dimensional world.

Graphics Card
Controls the display of pictures on the monitor. Also known as a video card.

GUI (Graphical User Interface)
A way of controlling a computer by choosing from a selection of windows, icons, and menus, rather than by typing in lines of code and commands. Microsoft's Windows and Apple's OS 8 are examples of graphical user interfaces.

H

Hardware
The physical parts of the computer, such as the monitor, printer, modem, and so on.

Hard Disk
A disk drive that can store a great deal of information, such as copies of all the documents or files you create. Hard disks are normally located inside a computer's casing, unlike a floppy disk which can be removed and easily transported.

Highlight
If you select a word from a menu it becomes highlighted – the word normally becomes white on a dark background.

High-density CD
A CD-ROM that can hold many times more data than the original CD-ROM.

Home Shopping
A service offered on interactive television systems and the Internet. It enables customers to view a graphical display of products for sale and make purchases simply by pressing a button on a handset.

Hot Spot
An on-screen button or picture in a multimedia title that reacts when you select it, often transporting you to another part of the title.

Hot Text
Hot text is highlighted on-screen text that, when selected, calls up related information or links you to another part of that title.

HTML
An abbreviation for Hypertext Markup Language. HTML is the set of text codes that indicates to a Web browser how to display the different elements of a Web page.

Hybrid CD-ROM
A CD-ROM that combines multimedia software with on-line features. Users with Internet access can connect to the World Wide Web directly from a hybrid CD-ROM's user interface.

Hypermedia
A collective term that describes the interactive elements of multimedia software, such as hot text and hot spots.

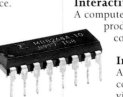
Sony PlayStation Console

RAM Chip

Hypertext
A body of text where some or all of the information is linked; so that when you, for example, click on a word you can find out more about that word or be transported to another area of the document that contains related information.

I

IBM-compatible PC
A PC (personal computer) that can run the same software as a PC from the IBM corporation (inventors of the original IBM PC).

CPU Chip

Icon
A pictorial representation of a computer file, program, feature, or function within a computer program or graphical user interface.

Image Manipulation Software
Used by multimedia designers to alter the appearance of images, such as photographs, once they have been scanned into a computer. Also known as imaging software.

Information Superhighway
A worldwide communications network that promises to bring multimedia services into the user's home via high-capacity fiber-optic cable. The Internet is sometimes seen as a prototype for the information superhighway. Also known simply as the superhighway.

Input Device
A device with which the user can transmit commands to the computer – a keyboard, mouse, trackball, and joystick are just a few examples.

I/O (Input/Output)
Input means to feed information into the computer; output is both the process of getting information out of the computer and the information that comes out, such as a printout or the information displayed on a monitor.

I/O Port
A connector that lets you attach cables to a computer in order to connect it to external devices such as a printer, a scanner, or an external modem.

ISDN
An abbreviation for Integrated Services Digital Network. ISDN is a communications standard that can carry voice and digital data at a rate of 64 kilobytes/second over a telephone line.

Interactive
A computer program, game, or any other product is interactive when the user can control what is displayed on-screen.

Interactive Television
A service that offers digital multimedia content on a television set, such as video-on-demand, on-line games, and home shopping.

Interface
The way two things work together. For example, the user interface refers to the way the user works with a computer, whereas the hardware interface describes the connectors that allow a computer to work with other hardware devices.

Internet
A worldwide network of computer networks, linking universities, commercial organizations, and private individuals. It offers access to the World Wide Web, e-mail, and other services.

JK

Java
A programming language used, among other things, for creating interactive applications that work over the Internet.

Joypad
A handheld controller with a number of control buttons and a directional pad that is used mainly for playing games.

Joystick
A hand-held column, used mainly for playing games, that controls the movement of objects on the screen.

Keyboard
An array of alphabetic and numeric keys that enables the user to type information into the computer.

Mouse

Keypad
Any small group of keys used for a special purpose. For example, a numeric keypad is used for entering lists of numbers.

Kilobyte
A unit of measure for binary data. Equivalent to roughly a thousand bytes.

Kiosk
A computer system, found in public places, that provides information and/or helps to sell goods.

M

Megabyte
Equivalent to roughly a thousand kilobytes.

Menu
A drop-down list of commands or functions. Choosing an item on the list activates that command, such as opening a file, for example.

Microprocessor
A chip that processes commands.

MIDI
Musical Instrument Digital Interface is a code that gives musical instructions, allowing a computer to create, record, and play back electronic music.

MMX
A special type of PC processor that has a set of extra instructions for handling multimedia data.

Modeling Software
Used by multimedia designers to create three-dimensional objects and images.

MPEG Compression
A compression standard developed by the Motion Picture Experts Group, designed for compressing digital video files.

Modem
A device that enables computers to communicate with each other over a telephone line.

Monitor
A piece of equipment that houses the computer screen. Also known as a display, or a VDU (Visual Display Unit).

Motion Capture
A technique used to record human movements in order to create lifelike animation.

Mouse
A hand-controlled input and pointing device. As the mouse is moved, it moves a cursor or pointer on the computer screen.

Multimedia
The inclusion of two or more media in a single application.

N

Navigation
The process of finding your way around the contents of a multimedia title.

Network
A group of two or more computers (and other devices, such as printers) that are linked together by some form of cable. A network may be in the same room, or it may be a larger system that connects computers all over the world.

O

On-line
Generally this refers to communication with other computers via a modem or network. The Internet provides multimedia on-line; a CD-ROM, by contrast, delivers multimedia off-line.

Joystick

On-line Services
Commercial services that can be accessed over a telephone line using a modem. They offer services such as e-mail, on-line encyclopedias, electronic newspapers and magazines, and hotel and airline reservation systems.

OS (Operating System)
The software that manages the essential operations of a computer, such as the display, organization of files, and communication with devices such as disk drives and sound cards. All computers need an operating system in order to

function. UNIX, Apple's OS 8, and Microsoft's DOS and Windows are examples of operating systems.

OCR (Optical Character Recognition)
A system of translating scanned text into a form that can be edited by a computer.

P

PC (Personal Computer)
A small computer designed for a single user. Technically, a PC refers to any brand of personal computer – however, many people use the term to refer to an IBM-compatible PC.

Pixel
Short for picture element, a pixel is one of the little dots of light that make up the picture on a computer screen. The greater the number of pixels in a given area, the higher the resolution.

Modem

Pixelation
The blocky effect that sometimes occurs during a digital video sequence, because the compression system cannot keep up with a particularly fast-moving section of the image.

Platform Game
A computer game where players have to jump from platform to platform, collecting various items, or fighting an enemy.

Plug-in
A small add-on program that works in conjunction with a Web browser and increases the range of file formats the browser can handle. Most plug-ins can be downloaded from the Web on demand.

Pointer
The shape that moves on the screen when you move the mouse. Some common shapes are the arrow, the hand, and the "I-beam."

Printer
An output device that prints information onto paper.

Program
A list of computer commands that perform a specific function. A multimedia title is a type of program, as are word processing and image manipulation applications.

Plug-and-play
Something is "plug-and-play" when it can be plugged in and used immediately, without a complicated set-up procedure. For example, a plug-and-play CD-ROM drive can be connected to a compatible computer and used right away. A plug-and-play operating system is one that can automatically recognize and set up external devices that are attached to a computer. The Apple Macintosh and some PCs are plug-and-play computers.

QR

RAM (Random Access Memory)
Memory chips that store information which can be easily read from or written to.

ROM (Read-Only Memory)
A storage device that can be read from but not written to. The most common examples are CD-ROMs and certain memory chips.

Rendering
The process in which a computer calculates a final image of a three-dimensional wireframe model, drawing in the surfaces, textures, and lighting chosen by the designer.

Resolution
The density of pixels that are used to make up an image on a computer.

RISC
An abbreviation for Reduced Instruction Set Computing – a new generation of processor chips that carry only a limited number of commands for faster operation.

S

Scanner
A device, similar to a photocopier, that creates electronic versions of photographs, drawings, and text. To store a picture on a computer, a scanner divides the image into a series of small dots and then processes them into digital bits of information.

Seek Time
The length of time it takes to access data on a hard disk or CD-ROM. The lower the seek time, the faster the information can be located.

Search Engine
Software that searches databases of Web sites and documents, according to criteria entered by a user, and displays the results as hypertext.

Server
A large computer that acts as a central file-storage area and forms part of a network.

Service Provider
A company that offers access to the Internet or an on-line service. Customers use a modem to connect to the service provider's computer, which has a permanent connection to the Internet or on-line service.

Set-top Box
A device that plugs into a television set and acts as a receiver and decoder of the digital information that comes into the home via telephone lines, cable, or satellite.

Streaming
A continuous-delivery technology for sending large files over the Internet. Streaming avoids lengthy download times and enables a sound or animation clip to be seen or heard almost immediately.

Software
A series of instructions for a computer that tell the computer what to do. For example, a multimedia title consists of software stored on a CD-ROM. A program is a piece of software.

Sound Card
An expansion card that allows the user to hear high-quality sound playback. It can also take sound from a microphone and convert it into a sound file for storage.

Sprite
An animated cut-out character or object that can be moved independently of the background in computer animation.

Stereoscopic Headset
A headset worn by users of virtual reality that helps to create the illusion of being in a three-dimensional world. The headset contains a small screen for each eye.

Surfing
The activity of navigating through documents on the World Wide Web via a succession of hypermedia.

Joypad

T

Telecommuters
A term used to describe people who work from home by connecting their home computer to their office computer via a modem or network. Also known as teleworkers.

Touch Screen
A computer screen with an electrically charged, conductive surface that allows the user to interact with it by the use of his or her finger rather than a mouse.

Trackball
A device that lets you control the cursor by rolling a stationary ball around with your fingers. Often used on portable computers where there is no desk space for a mouse.

Transfer Rate
The rate at which data is transferred from one computer to another, or from a disk drive or CD-ROM drive to the computer.

UV

URL
An abbreviation for Uniform Resource Locator (or Universal Resource Locator). A URL is the unique location of a document on the Internet.

Virtual Reality
A situation in which a computer is used to create an illusion of reality by simulating a three-dimensional environment.

Voice Recognition
A computer system designed to recognize and act upon the human voice.

VRML
An abbreviation for Virtual Reality Modelling Language. A VRML is a development tool used by designers to create interactive 3-D animations for the Web.

W

Wavetable
The bank of digitized sounds, sampled from real instruments and sounds, that is found on some sound cards. Used in the creation of MIDI music.

Web Browser
A program used to view information on the World Wide Web.

Web Site
A computer or server that stores documents which can be accessed via the World Wide Web. Sometimes used to refer to a collection of Web pages.

Web Page
A single page of a Web site, built using HTML, and which may display a variety of multimedia elements.

Window
A rectangular frame on the screen that contains specific information. For example, one window might contain a multimedia program, while another might contain a list of files.

Wireframe
A way of representing three-dimensional shapes when designing computer graphics. Objects are drawn as if they were built out of wires, without complex shading or textures.

Workstation
A computer that is far more powerful and much more expensive than a personal computer. Most workstations contain special-purpose graphics hardware and are used for animation, software development, and computer-aided design.

World Wide Web
A hypertext-based system for finding and accessing information on the Internet. The World Wide Web consists of a series of "pages" of information, many of which contain text, color graphics, and even sound and video clips.

INDEX

ACKNOWLEDGMENTS

The publisher would like to thank the following copyright holders for their kind permission to reproduce their screengrabs, all of which are trademarks.

a=above; b=below; c=center; l=left; r=right; t=top.

Activision: 93bl; Adobe: 60bl, 131t, br, 133br, c, 135cl, bca, bl, 145tr, 151bl, bc, 154tr, 155cr; American Red Cross: 168crb; Apple Computer Inc: 90tr, cb, 91ca, 172bl; Argonaut Software Ltd, London: 46bc, br, 95c, 146–147; Atari: 8bl, br, 92c, cr, br, 93clb, br, 175bc; BBC Online: 169br; BMG Interactive: 17crb, 29br, 57, 93bc, 122clb; Boosey and Hawkes Music Publishers Ltd: 129ca; Broderbund Software Ltd: 17tr, tcb, cr, 34–35, 36, 44–45, 142tc; BSkyB: 160cb; Bullfrog Productions Ltd: 48, 102cb, 148–149; Cakewalk Music Software: 128cra, 129tl, cl, cla; "Official Grand Canyon Tourism" www://thecanyon.com courtesy of Canyon WebWorks and Multimedia: 31 br; Cambridge Display Technology Ltd: 179br; Citibank: 169tl; © 1998 Cable News Network, Inc. All rights reserved. Used by permission of CNN: 168tr; CompuServe Incorporated: 88ca, 172; Tomb Raider II © and ™ 1997 Core Design Ltd © and P 1997 Eidos Interactive Limited. All Rights Reserved: 17clb, 47, 70tr, cr; Screen shots taken from 3D Atlas courtesy of Creative Wonders. © 1997 Creative Wonders. All rights reserved: 24-25; CRT Multimedia: 61; Digidesign: 123bl, 127c, 126; Disc Manufacturing Inc: 81cr; Division Ltd: 103clb, 105tl, cl, bl; DKFL: 36; © 1994/1995 Domestic Funk Products: 116br, 117tl, tr, clb, br, 118tr, c, br, 119t, tr; Electronic Arts: 16crb, 19trb, 99c, 112–113, 114–115, 150cb, 156b; EuroTalk: Heinemann International 40b, © Les Editions Albert René, Goscinny-Uderzo 40–41c, 41t; Europress Software: 39c, bc, br; Fractal Design Corporation: Painter & Natural Media™ 131cra, 132–133; France Telecom Intelmatique: 172cr; Doug Gaerlan and Madu Siddlingaian:171cr; The Gap: 169tc, 171bl; General Magic: 179tr, ca; id software: 12bl, 46c 50–51; IVI Publishing: 13cr, 19bcr, br, 157br; Knowledge Adventure: 17tc, JumpStart Kindergarten, courtesy of Knowledge Adventure Inc. ™ and © 1994 Knowledge Adventure Inc. All rights

reserved: 32–33; Spider-Man Cartoon Maker, courtesy of Knowledge Adventure, Inc © 1995 Knowledge Adventure Inc. All rights reserved. ™ and © Marvel Characters, Inc. All rights reserved: 17ca, 39t; The Learning Company: 58, 75c, French Vocabulary Builder © The Learning Company 1995. All Rights Reserved: 17tcb, 41b; Courtesy of LucasArts Entertainment Company: Dark Forces ™ and © 1994 Lucasfilm Ltd: 12br, 102cr, 143b, /Full Throttle ® & © 1994 LucasArts Entertainment Company.17c, 52tr, c, r, 53, 142c, cr, /© 1993 LucasArts Entertainment Company. 142b; X-Wing © 1992 Lucasfilm Ltd. 143cb, All Rights Reserved. Used Under Authorization; © 1998 Lycos, Inc. Lycos ® is a registered trademark of Carnegie Mellon University. All rights reserved: 168–169c; 1996 Macromedia Inc. All rights reserved. Shockwave is a trademark of Macromedia Inc: 110cra, 117cl, c, bl, bc, 116br, 118cl, cb, b, 119c, ca, 121cl, c, 123bc, 127tc, 145bl, 151br; MicroProse: 49cl, c, cr, br, /Spectrum Holobyte 54–55; MSN is a trademark and Microsoft, MS-DOS, and Windows are registered trademarks of Microsoft Corporation. Screenshots reprinted with permission from Microsoft Corporation: 13cr, 16cr, 20–21, 26–27, 31t, c, bl, 38, 70car, cl, 80bc, 86c, br, 87ca, cb, 89b, 120bc, br, 163, 167tr, 169crb, 172br, bc; Mirage Technologies (Multimedia) Ltd: 143tr, cr; Mountain Journeys: 169ca; Muze Inc: 64tr; NASA: 12tr, 167bl, c, 168bc; Copyright 1996 Netscape Communications Corp. All Rights Reserved. This page may not be reprinted or copied without the express written permission of Netscape: 167br; Nintendo: 65c, 93tr, cb, 101; Notting Hill Electronic Publishing: 43t; Photos courtesy of the Open University's Knowledge Media Institute: 168cl; Philips Interactive: 94ca, 96tr, 97br; Pixsys/Image Guided Technology: 136br; PointCast: 169bl; Quark Inc: 91tr; ©Real Networks: 170; Courtesy of Rollerblade, Inc: 169c; Sega and SEGA SATURN are trademarks of SEGA ENTERPRISES, Ltd: 92tc, 93ca, 95b, 97; 7th Level: 58tr, 59; Sierra On-Line: 17cl, 52bc, 56bl, l, 57; Softkey International: 19bl; Sony Interactive, Europe:/Naughty Dog: 98bl, /Psygnosis: 99crb, 122cl, /Square Soft: 98br; Specula International: 13cb, 137, 138–139; ©Superscape: 171cb; Used by permission of

Sun Microsystems Inc. Copyright 1997 Sun Microsystems, Inc. 2550 Garcia Ave. Mtn. View, CA 94043-1100 USA, All rights reserved: 162bc; Tesco Direct: 169tr; Time Warner Cable's Full Service Network, a division of Time Warner Entertainment Co., L.P. 11cr, bl, 12tcr, 174tc, bc, 175tr, crb, 177c; ©1992 Turner Music Publishing, Inc. All Rights Reserved: 127tl; Virgin Interactive Entertainment: 19cra, 119br, /Looking Glass Technology 49t, / © Virgin Interactive Entertainment, Inc. All Rights Reserved. Created by Mechadeus 56bl, 151tr, 153tc, b; Virgin Net: 170br; Virtuality Entertainment: 80br, 104; Voyager: 18bl, cr, br, 19c, cl, cr, crb; The White House: 168bl; World Wide Fund for Nature: 168br; Wienerworld Interactive/Graphix Zone: 157cl; Xebec Multi Media Solutions: 17bc, 60bl.

The publishers would like to thank the following for their kind permission to reproduce their photographs.
Bridgeman Art Library, London: Self Portrait as a Young Man 1634 by Rembrandt 9tr; British Airways: 17bcl, 64cr, br, bc, 65b; BT Corporate Picture Library; a BT photograph: 13bl, 160b,168br, 172; Compaq Computer Corporation: 88bc; The Computer Museum, Boston: 84bl, 84cr; Encyclopaedia Britannica International Ltd: 9br; Government Centre for Information Systems Library, Norwich: 63tl; Hutchison: 161br; IBM: 82cb, 83tc, bl, 86bl; Microsoft Corporation/Text 100: 86cla; NASA: 161bl; Science Photo Library: 71bc, 74tr, 83cb; Smithsonian Institution: 17bcr, 62; Sony: 75br; Telegraph Colour Library: 122t; Woodfin Camp: Jim Wilson 84ca; Xerox PARC/ Brian Tramontana 85br; Zefa Pictures: 160t.

Jacket
CompuServe Incorporated: front & back crb, tlb; Electronic Arts: front & back bl, bcl, clb; Courtesy of Rollerblade, Inc.: cla; SEGA Enterprises, Ltd: front & back; Sony Interactive, Europe/Square Soft: front & back tl.

Dorling Kindersley would like to thank the following people for their help in producing this book: Angus Beare, Bill Cooper, Jason Cyphus, Richard Evans, Sion King, William Tyler, Sam Segar, and Dalwinder Singh.